CliffsNotes

Creating Your First Web Page

By Alan Simpson

IN THIS BOOK

- Install and use the free Web authoring software FrontPage Express
- Write text, insert graphics, and edit your first Web page
- Create links to other Internet resources and to other pages within your Web site
- Publish your pages and promote your Web site
- Reinforce what you learn with CliffsNotes Review
- Find more Web publishing information in CliffsNotes Resource Center and online at www.cliffsnotes.com

IDG Books Worldwide, Inc.
An International Data Group Company
Foster City, CA • Chicago, IL • Indianapolis, IN • New York, NY

IDG
BOOKS
WORLDWIDE

About the Author

Alan Simpson's more than 75 computer-related books on topics including the Internet, operating systems, databases, and Web authoring have sold millions of copies throughout the world. Alan is also the author of the popular www.coolnerds.com Web site, has taught programming courses at San Diego State University and the University of California San Diego Extension, and has served as a freelance consultant and programmer.

Publisher's Acknowledgments

Editorial

Project Editor: Jeanne S. Criswell, M.F.A.

Acquisitions Editor: Andy Cummings

Copy Editors: Ted Cains, Constance Carlisle

Technical Editors: James Michael Stewart, Michael Lerch

Editorial Assistant: Jamila Pree

Production

Proofreader: York Production Services

Indexer: York Production Services

IDG Books Indianapolis Production Department

CliffsNotes™ Creating Your First Web Page
Published by
IDG Books Worldwide, Inc.
An International Data Group Company
919 E. Hillsdale Blvd.
Suite 400
Foster City, CA 94404
www.idgbooks.com (IDG Books Worldwide Web site)
www.cliffsnotes.com (CliffsNotes Web site)

Library of Congress Catalog Card No.: 99-64198

ISBN: 0-7645-8520-7

Printed in the United States of America

10 9 8 7 6 5 4 3 2 1

1O/RS/QY/ZZ/IN

Distributed in the United States by IDG Books Worldwide, Inc.

Distributed by CDG Books Canada Inc. for Canada; by Transworld Publishers Limited in the United Kingdom; by IDG Norge Books for Norway; by IDG Sweden Books for Sweden; by IDG Books Australia Publishing Corporation Pty. Ltd. for Australia and New Zealand; by TransQuest Publishers Pte Ltd. for Singapore, Malaysia, Thailand, Indonesia, and Hong Kong; by Gotop Information Inc. for Taiwan; by ICG Muse, Inc. for Japan; by Norma Comunicaciones S.A. for Colombia; by Intersoft for South Africa; by Eyrolles for France; by International Thomson Publishing for Germany, Austria and Switzerland; by Distribuidora Cuspide for Argentina; by Livraria Cultura for Brazil; by Ediciones ZETA S.C.R. Ltda. for Peru; by WS Computer Publishing Corporation, Inc., for the Philippines; by Contemporanea de Ediciones for Venezuela; by Express Computer Distributors for the Caribbean and West Indies; by Micronesia Media Distributor, Inc. for Micronesia; by Grupo Editorial Norma S.A. for Guatemala; by Chips Computadoras S.A. de C.V. for Mexico; by Editorial Norma de Panama S.A. for Panama; by American Bookshops for Finland. Authorized Sales Agent: Anthony Rudkin Associates for the Middle East and North Africa.

For general information on IDG Books Worldwide's books in the U.S., please call our Consumer Customer Service department at 800-762-2974. For reseller information, including discounts and premium sales, please call our Reseller Customer Service department at 800-434-3422.

For information on where to purchase IDG Books Worldwide's books outside the U.S., please contact our International Sales department at 317-596-5530 or fax 317-596-5692.

For consumer information on foreign language translations, please contact our Customer Service department at 1-800-434-3422, fax 317-596-5692, or e-mail rights@idgbooks.com.

For information on licensing foreign or domestic rights, please phone +1-650-655-3109.

For sales inquiries and special prices for bulk quantities, please contact our Sales department at 650-655-3200 or write to the address above.

For information on using IDG Books Worldwide's books in the classroom or for ordering examination copies, please contact our Educational Sales department at 800-434-2086 or fax 317-596-5499.

For press review copies, author interviews, or other publicity information, please contact our Public Relations department at 650-655-3000 or fax 650-655-3299.

For authorization to photocopy items for corporate, personal, or educational use, please contact Copyright Clearance Center, 222 Rosewood Drive, Danvers, MA 01923, or fax 978-750-4470.

Table of Contents

INTRODUCTION

Welcome to CliffsNotes *Creating Your First Web Page*, the fastest way to get from being a spectator to being a published author on the World Wide Web. While many tools are available for creating Web pages, I use FrontPage Express in this book for four reasons:

- FrontPage Express is easy to learn and easy to use.

- FrontPage Express is powerful.

- FrontPage Express is free.

- The skills you build with FrontPage Express also apply to other Web tools!

Microsoft FrontPage Express is actually a scaled-down version of the Microsoft commercial product Microsoft FrontPage. Although the Express version doesn't offer all the bells and whistles that FrontPage offers, it still provides enough functionality to create great-looking Web pages with minimal fuss. With FrontPage Express, you can create Web pages with pictures, hyperlinks, tables, background music, and other cool stuff, without getting bogged down in the intricacies of HTML (the language used to build Web pages).

Why Do You Need This Book?

Can you answer yes to any of these questions?

- Do you need to learn about creating a Web page fast?

- Don't have time to read 500 pages about Web publishing?

- Do you want to keep your out-of-pocket expenses to an absolute minimum?

■ Are you perplexed by all the technical terms and buzzwords used in Web publishing?

■ Do you want to focus on the creative aspects, rather than the technical aspects, of creating Web pages?

If so, then CliffsNotes *Creating Your First Web Page* is for you!

How to Use This Book

You're the boss — you decide how to use this book. You can either read the book from cover to cover or just look for the information you want and then put the book back on the shelf for later. However, I recommend here a few ways to search for your topic(s).

■ Use the index in the back of the book to find what you're looking for.

■ Flip through the book looking for your topic in the running heads.

■ Look for your topic in the table of contents in the front of the book.

■ Look at the "In This Chapter" list at the beginning of each chapter.

■ Look for additional information in the CliffsNotes Resource Center.

■ Flip through the book until you find what you're looking for because the book is organized in a logical, task-oriented way.

I also put some icons next to choice chunks of text so that you can find important information quickly. Here is a description of the icons you find in the book.

If you see a Remember icon, make a mental note because this text is worth keeping in mind.

If you see a Tip icon, you know that you've run across a helpful hint, uncovered a secret, or received helpful advice.

If you see a Warning icon, you need to watch out for something that can be dangerous, requires special caution, or should be avoided.

Don't Miss Our Web Site

Keep up with the changing world of the Internet by visiting the CliffsNotes Web site at www.cliffsnotes.com. Here's what you find:

- Interactive tools that are fun and informative
- Links to interesting Web sites
- Additional resources to help you continue your learning

At www.cliffsnotes.com, you can even register for a new feature called CliffsNotes Daily, which offers you newsletters on a variety of topics, delivered right to your e-mail inbox each business day.

If you haven't yet discovered the Internet and are wondering how to get online, pick up *Getting On the Internet*, new from CliffsNotes. You'll learn just what you need to make your online connection quickly and easily. See you at www.cliffsnotes.com!

CHAPTER 1

PREPARING TO CREATE

IN THIS CHAPTER

- Installing your free Web authoring tools
- Configuring your system
- Getting started with FrontPage Express

Creating Web pages, like anything else, requires two ingredients: skills and tools. In this chapter, I briefly discuss the skills you should already have when starting this book and then focus on getting all your Web authoring tools together. You also learn how to set up some programs and shortcuts on your PC to simplify and streamline your Web authoring efforts.

What You Should Already Know

In this book, I assume that you aren't an absolute beginner on a PC. You should already have experience using Windows and know the basics of clicking, double-clicking, right-clicking, and so forth. You don't need to be a Windows guru. The absolute basics of using the Windows Start menu and desktop, an understanding of folders and files, and the ability to open and close programs and documents should be sufficient. Likewise, you should know some rudimentary word processing and understand the basics of text editing.

I also assume that you've been on the Web and know what a Web page looks like. You *don't* need to know about Web authoring tools, such as FrontPage Express, nor do you need to know how to publish to the Web. I cover all that in this book. But you should already have a sense of what a Web page looks like and perhaps even some ideas about what you want to present on your Web pages.

Tools You Need

To best use your time while you learn to create your Web pages, you want to use the most modern tools available. Windows 98 provides those tools in the form of Microsoft FrontPage Express, Web Publishing Wizard, and Personal Web Server. If you're using Windows 95 or some earlier version of Windows, upgrading now is well worth the effort — not only to help you use this book, but also to streamline your entire Web publishing effort.

The authoring tools I discuss in this book are also part of the Microsoft Internet Explorer package, which you can download from www.microsoft.com/ie. Also, I discuss the Internet Tools that come with Version 5 of Microsoft Internet Explorer. If you notice any discrepancies between the tools you're using and the tools in this book, you may want to download Version 5 of Internet Explorer. Doing so doesn't take that long and won't cost you a cent.

Web sites change. As a result, you may not find what you're looking for at the URLs presented in this chapter. As an alternative, you can check the pages at www.microsoft.com/msdownload and http://windowsupdate.microsoft.com for the latest versions of programs discussed in this chapter.

Setting Up Your Authoring Environment

In this book, I assume that you plan to use Microsoft FrontPage Express as your main tool to author your Web pages. Two related Internet tools that can also help are Microsoft's Web Publishing Wizard and Personal Web Server (PWS). All three tools are freebies that come with Windows 98, as well as with Microsoft Internet Explorer.

Before you launch into creating your first Web page, you can take some steps to set up your PC as an ideal Web authoring tool. These steps include making sure that you have all the right programs installed and configured correctly. Also, you can set up some shortcuts to simplify accessing these programs and the pages you plan to create. You need to do all these things only once — not each time you want to work on your Web site. So start by getting all your Web authoring ducks in a row, beginning with making sure that FrontPage Express and the Web Publishing Wizard are installed by following these steps:

1. Click the Windows Start button.

2. Choose Programs⇨Internet Explorer to reveal its submenu. If you see FrontPage Express and Web Publishing Wizard on the submenu, as in Figure 1-1, you already have those programs installed, and you can skip to the section titled "Installing Personal Web Server."

If you don't see FrontPage Express and Web Publishing Wizard on the Internet Explorer menu, follow these steps to check the Internet Tools menu under Accessories:

1. Click the Start button.

2. Choose Programs⇨Accessories⇨Internet Tools to view its submenu.

If you do see FrontPage Express and Web Publishing Wizard on the menu that appears, skip to the section titled "Installing Personal Web Server." Otherwise, continue reading to install FrontPage Express and Web Publishing Wizard.

Figure 1-1: FrontPage Express and Web Publishing Wizard are already installed.

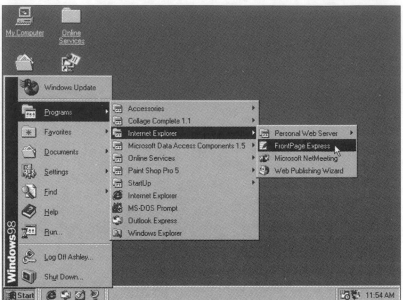

Installing the authoring tools

If FrontPage Express and Web Publishing Wizard aren't on your computer, you can easily install them from your Windows 98 CD-ROM by following these steps:

1. Click the Windows Start button.

2. Choose Settings⇨Control Panel.

3. Double-click the Add/Remove Programs icon.

4. Click the Windows Setup tab.

5. Click Internet Tools and then click the Details button. The Internet Tools dialog box appears.

6. If you need to install FrontPage Express, click its check box at the top of the list of components that appears, as shown in Figure 1-2.

Figure 1-2:   Check FrontPage Express to install it.

7. If you need to install Web Publishing Wizard, scroll down to the bottom of the list of components and select the check box next to Web Publishing Wizard.

8. Click OK at the bottom of the Internet Tools dialog box.

9. Click OK at the bottom of the Add/Remove Programs dialog box.

10. Follow the instructions that appear on the screen.

When the installation finishes, close out of the Control Panel window. You're ready to install the last component you need, Microsoft Personal Web Server.

Installing Personal Web Server

A *Web server* is a program that you use on an Internet server computer to publish Web pages. Microsoft Personal Web Server (PWS) is a scaled-down program that makes your personal computer mimic a true Web server. Essentially, PWS enables you to create and test Web pages on your own PC prior to publishing them on the Web. Typically, you have to install and configure PWS before you can use it. You only need to perform the installation once.

To install Personal Web Server, you need your original Windows 98 CD-ROM. Insert the CD into your CD-ROM drive. If a window titled Windows 98 CD-ROM appears automatically, just close that window. Then install Personal Web Server by following these steps:

1. Choose Start⇨Run.

2. Type **d:\add-ons\pws\setup.exe**. (You need to replace **d** with the letter of your CD-ROM drive, if it isn't drive D.)

3. Click OK. The Microsoft Personal Web Server Setup window appears.

4. Click Next. You see three buttons labeled Minimum, Typical, and Custom.

5. Click the Typical button.

6. On the next screen, shown in Figure 1-3, leave the settings as they are so that your Web publishing home directory is C:\Inetpub\wwwroot.

7. Click Next. You see a window that monitors the progress of the PWS files as they're copied to your hard disk. When that process is complete, you see a Thank you... message.

Figure 1-3: Use C:\Inetpub\wwwroot as your default Web publishing home directory.

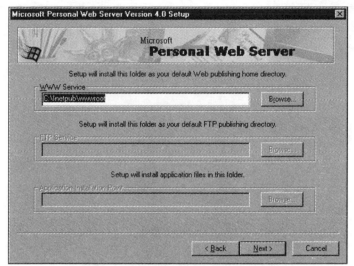

8. Click the Finish button near the bottom of the window. After a brief delay, you see a window asking if you want to restart your computer. Remove the CD from your CD-ROM drive (and any disks you may have put in floppy drives) and then click the Yes button.

After your computer restarts, you notice a new icon on the desktop labeled Publish. You also see a tiny icon in the indicators section of the taskbar down near the lower-right corner of the screen. If you point to that icon, you see the message `Personal Web Server is running`, as shown in Figure 1-4. You won't notice any other changes to your system. In fact, everything works just as it always did. As you discover in Chapter 2, Personal Web Server enables you, or anyone in your local area network, to view your page in any Web browser.

Figure 1-4: The icon indicates that Personal Web Server is running.

Configuring Personal Web Server

After you install Personal Web Server (PWS), you need to make a small adjustment to its default settings. Here's why. Your *Web presence provider* (WPP) — the company that makes your Web pages accessible to everyone on the Internet — may require that you give your site's home page a specific name, typically index.html. You want to configure PWS so that it uses the same default home page name that your Web presence provider requires. If you haven't found a Web presence provider yet, chances are whomever you choose will require that you name your home page index.html. If you do have a Web presence provider already, and you know for certain that the provider requires something other than index.html, use the provider's required name.

To set the default home page name in Personal Web Server, follow these steps:

1. Double-click the Personal Web Server icon in the Windows taskbar near the lower-right corner of your screen.

2. If the Tip of the Day window appears, click its Close button. The Personal Web Manager window remains on the screen, as shown in Figure 1-5.

3. Note the blue underlined URLs that appear in the window. The first is the location of your home page. That location is `http://computername,` where *computername* is the name of the computer you're using (*poweredge* in the example). The path shown, typically

Figure 1-5:   The Personal Web Manager window is open on the desktop.

C:\Inetpub\wwwroot, is where you store Web pages, including any pictures. You may want to jot down on a scratch piece of paper both the URL and path, for future reference.

4. Click the Advanced icon near the lower-left corner of the Personal Web Manager window.

5. Make sure that the Enable Default Document check box, shown in Figure 1-6, contains a check mark.

6. Change the name of the Default Document(s) to **index.html** (all lowercase letters) as in Figure 1-6 — unless you know for sure that your Web presence provider requires some other name, in which case substitute that name for index.html.

7. Close the Personal Web Manager window.

Figure 1-6: Change the Default Document(s) entry to index.html.

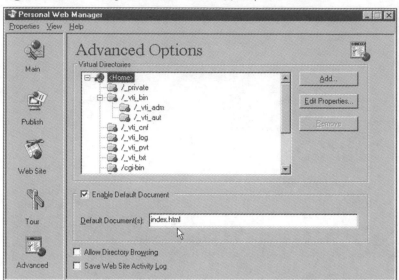

You've completed the installations necessary to use FrontPage Express and related tools to author your Web pages. I suggest that you spend a few minutes setting up some shortcuts and tweaking a few Windows settings to further simplify your work.

Simplifying Your System

Beyond installing and configuring required programs, you may want to set up some shortcuts to the resources you use most while authoring Web pages. Setting everything up only takes a few minutes, and you only need to do these things once. Here, I give you three tips for setting up your authoring environment, which can save you lots of time.

Making a shortcut to your Web folder

To give yourself quick access to the files that make up your Web site, you can create a desktop shortcut to your C:\Inetpub\ wwwroot folder. Doing so enables you to open that folder without going through My Computer or Windows Explorer. Just use whatever technique you prefer for creating desktop shortcuts in Windows.

Customizing your SendTo menu

Normally, when you open a Web page in Windows, the page appears in your Web browser. This arrangement is fine for viewing the page, but not necessarily for editing it. If you add FrontPage Express to your SendTo menu, you can bypass the browser and send any HTML file right into FrontPage Express. Just right-click any Web page and choose SendTo⇔ FrontPage Express, as shown in Figure 1-7.

Figure 1-7:   Customize the SendTo menu to allow quick access to FrontPage Express.

To add FrontPage Express to your SendTo menu, follow these steps:

1. In Windows Explorer, locate the FrontPage Express application. It's probably in your Program Files folder inside the Microsoft FrontPage Express folder. Make sure that the application is displayed in the right pane of Windows Explorer.

2. In the left pane of Windows Explorer, click the plus sign next to the Windows folder on your C drive. You see a list of folders appear beneath the Windows folder, including the SendTo folder. Do *not* click on the SendTo folder.

3. Back in the right pane of Windows Explorer, right-click on the FrontPage Express application and drag the icon to the SendTo folder in the left pane.

4. Release the mouse button.

5. Choose Create Shortcut(s) Here from the popup menu that appears. Windows creates a shortcut in the SendTo folder. Just for giggles, you can check this by clicking the SendTo folder to display its contents.

6. If you want to change the name of the shortcut, just right-click on the shortcut, choose Rename from the popup menu, and type in the new name.

You can also add Web browsers, graphics programs, and other favorite programs to your SendTo menu.

Unhiding your filename extensions

As you may know, Windows uses filename extensions to associate documents with programs. For example, Web pages are generally saved with the filename extension htm or html.

When you click on a file that has one of these extensions, Windows knows to open that page in your Web browser.

By default, Windows hides the filename extensions on files that are associated with specific programs. For example, if you create a Web page named index.html, then view that file's icon through My Computer, Windows Explorer, or Find, you may see only the filename, index. As a Web author, you probably want to see filename extensions while browsing around your computer, so that you can tell which files are HTML, GIF, or JPEG files. Just follow the normal Windows procedure for unhiding file extensions.

Starting FrontPage Express

Starting FrontPage Express is like starting any other program on your PC. After you create a desktop or Quick Launch toolbar icon for starting FrontPage Express, you can just double-click that icon. If you don't have a desktop icon for starting FrontPage Express, follow these steps instead:

1. Click the Windows Start button.

2. Choose Programs⇨Internet Explorer⇨FrontPage Express. Or if you don't find FrontPage Express there, try choosing Programs⇨Accessories⇨Internet Tools⇨FrontPage Express.

Like most Windows programs, FrontPage Express opens in its own window. You also see the standard components found in other Windows programs, including a title bar, menu bar, toolbar, main window or document area, and status bar, as shown in Figure 1-8.

Figure 1-8: FrontPage Express is open on the Windows desktop.

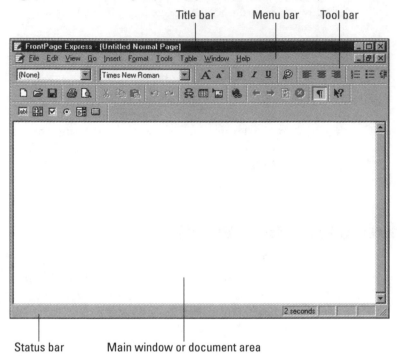

Status bar   Main window or document area

The toolbars in FrontPage Express provide quick access to frequently used program features. To see the name of any button on a toolbar, just point to the button. A tool tip showing the button's name appears near the mouse pointer.

To show or hide toolbars, open the FrontPage Express View menu. Toolbar names with check marks next to them are already on display. Click the name of any toolbar to hide it if it's checked or to show it if it's hidden.

Closing FrontPage Express

Closing FrontPage Express is no different than closing any other program. From the following list, choose the method that you find most convenient:

- Click the Close button near the upper-right corner of the FrontPage Express window.

- Choose File⇨Close from the FrontPage Express menu bar.

- Right-click the FrontPage Express taskbar button and choose Close.

- If FrontPage Express is in the active window, press Alt+F4.

Of course, if you leave any unsaved work behind, FrontPage Express gives you a chance to save that work before closing. You should always choose Yes when asked about saving your work, unless you're absolutely sure you want to scrap all the work you've done since you last saved the page.

Publishing Your Pages

You haven't created any pages yet, so you have nothing to publish at the moment. But to avoid any potential confusion or disappointment down the road, you need to know that just creating Web pages on your own PC doesn't make those pages accessible to people on the Internet. In fact, as long as the pages remain only on your PC, you (and perhaps other people on your local area network) are the only people capable of seeing those pages.

To make your Web pages visible to Internet users at large, you need to copy those completed pages to a *Web server*. In the "Installing Personal Web Server" section earlier in this chapter, I define *Web server* as a software program, such as Personal

Web Server (PWS); the term also applies to a computer that's connected to the Internet 24 hours a day, seven days a week, and capable of serving Web pages to anyone who requests them. (Blame the computer geeks for using the same name.)

If you already have access to the Internet, you need to find out whether or not your Internet service provider (ISP) includes *Web hosting* (the ability to publish your Web pages) as part of its service. If it doesn't, you may want to shop for a Web presence provider (WPP). Typically, a Web presence provider offers only space on a Web server. You can still use your existing ISP to browse the Web, do your e-mail, and all the normal things you do. You can upload your pages to the Web presence provider's server by using your existing ISP, even if your ISP and WPP are two entirely different companies.

If you don't have any place to publish your pages and are shopping around, you may want to look for a Web presence provider that supports Microsoft FrontPage Extensions. *Extensions* are small programs that exist on the Web server and provide added functionality. Microsoft FrontPage provides easy access to those extensions. FrontPage Express can also use a few of them. However, the extensions aren't too terribly important if you're using only FrontPage Express to create your Web pages — certainly not important enough to go to any added expense.

Nonetheless, if you're starting from scratch in looking for a Web presence provider, and you think that at some point you may want to start developing more complex Web sites using Microsoft FrontPage, the FrontPage Server Extensions are worth pursuing. To locate Web presence providers that offer FrontPage extensions, check out the following Web page: `www.microsoftwpp.com/wppsearch`.

CHAPTER 2

CREATING YOUR HOME PAGE

IN THIS CHAPTER

- Creating, titling, and naming your page
- Saving your page
- Adding and formatting text
- Looking at your page in a Web browser
- Looking at your page's HTML

Now that you've set up your PC as your personal Web authoring tool, you're ready to create your first Web page. In this chapter, you create the site's home page. As you may already know, a *home page* is simply the first page that a person comes to when visiting your site. For this example, I set up the home page of a hypothetical orchid club. Of course, you can use the techniques described here to put whatever content you want in your Web page.

Creating Your Home Page

To create your home page, open Microsoft FrontPage Express. Automatically, FrontPage Express displays a new, blank Web page titled Untitled Normal Page. Before you start typing any text, you need to title your page and save it so that it has a filename.

Titling your Web page

At some point, you will (presumably) publish your page on the World Wide Web. When search engines like Yahoo!, Excite, and others display information about your page, the main link to your page is its title. Therefore, you always want to give your page a good, descriptive title. This title doesn't appear anywhere within the page itself, only in search engines, in the title bar of FrontPage Express, and in the title bar of most Web browsers. To title your page, follow these steps:

1. From the FrontPage Express menu bar, choose File⇨Page Properties.

2. On the General tab, type a title in the Title text box.

3. Click OK.

You won't see any change to the page itself. However, the FrontPage Express title bar displays your page's title where it previously showed Untitled Normal Page.

Saving your page

Remember from Chapter 1 that your home page needs to have a specific name, as determined by your Internet service provider or whoever hosts your Web site. Typically, you need to name the home page index.html or index.htm. Remember that many Web servers are case-sensitive to filenames. So you have to use uppercase and lowercase letters consistently when referring to files. The almost universal guideline is never to use uppercase letters in filenames. Use only lowercase letters.

Also important is saving your home page in the default Web site defined by Personal Web Server. The name of that site is `http://computername`, where *computername* is the name of your computer. (In the example in Chapter 1, that name is `http://poweredge`.) FrontPage Express suggests this location by default, so you only need to remember *not* to change it. Here are the exact steps:

1. Click the Save button in the toolbar or choose File⇨Save from the FrontPage Express menu bar.

2. In the Save As dialog box that appears, *don't* change the page title.

3. Under Page Location, change the filename at the end of the pathname to index.html.

4. Click OK.

That's all you have to do. Now, whenever you want to save your work, you just have to click the Save button in the toolbar or choose File⇨Save from the menu bar; the page is saved instantly.

Adding Text to Your Web Page

With FrontPage Express, you can add and manipulate text for your Web page in much the same way that you add and manipulate text for documents in word processing programs. If you're at all familiar with Microsoft Word — and similar word processing programs — you should feel right at home.

If you need some help with the basic word processing skills, check out the *FrontPage 2000 Bible* (see the Resource Center at the back of this book); it goes into more detail about entering and formatting text in FrontPage.

When you're creating your Web page, FrontPage Express is creating an *HTML* (*Hypertext Markup Language*) document behind the scenes. HTML is the language that defines text formatting so that your Web page can appear on the World Wide Web. But with a few distinctions (which I point out, as appropriate), you can use standard word processing techniques to accomplish a variety of text actions, including the following:

- **Type text:** Just type as you do in most word processing programs. Use the Enter, Backspace, Delete, and other keys the same way, too.

- **Select text:** Use the mouse or the keyboard to select text. FrontPage Express works on the standard "select, then do" principle, which means you first identify the text you want to alter or format by selecting it and then click a toolbar button or make a menu selection to change it.

- **Move, copy, and delete text:** Just select the text and use the standard cut-and-paste techniques.

- **Format text:** Select the text and then change its appearance. You can make text larger or smaller; apply boldface, italics, or underline; align text to the left, right, or center; or change the text's color or font (print style). HTML provides many different formats (see Figure 2-1) that you can easily apply to your text using FrontPage Express.

You can also reverse a recent formatting change by pressing Ctrl+Z or choosing Edit⇨Undo from the FrontPage Express menu bar.

Make sure that you pick fonts that visitors to your Web site are likely to have installed on their computers. The reason is that only the instruction to use a particular font is passed on to visitors' PCs, not the font itself. If you use a font that's not on their machines, any text that uses that font may not appear correctly on-screen. Instead, the text may appear in whatever default font (usually Times Roman) their browsers use. Fortunately, most PCs have installed on them such basic fonts as Arial, Times Roman, and Courier.

Figure 2-1:   The Font dialog box in FrontPage Express.

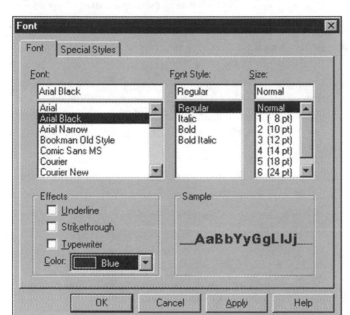

- **Size text:** Size text for your Web page, but keep in mind that font sizes for Web pages are assigned on a scale of 1 to 7 (smallest to largest). A size of 1 shows text at about 8 points; 7 shows text at about 36 points.

  To resize text, simply select it and click either the Increase Text Size or Decrease Text Size button on the toolbar. These buttons cycle your text through the seven predefined text sizes.

Warning

The standard method of assigning a specific point size to the text isn't reliable on the Internet because so many different types of computers can view the text. No one can guarantee that a particular person's PC can show the font at a specific point size.

In case you're new to fonts, a point is a unit of measurement that equals about ½ of an inch.

■ **Add a heading:** Apply a heading style as you apply any predefined formatting style to text. Simply use the Change Style drop-down list in the Format toolbar. But remember that HTML (hence, FrontPage Express) provides only six predefined heading styles, named Heading 1 through Heading 6, as shown in Figure 2-2.

■ **Insert special characters:** To insert special characters (such as © or Æ) into your Web page, place your cursor where you want the special character to appear, choose Insert⇨Symbol, and select the character you want to insert.

Figure 2-2: Headings and a few other predefined styles are available from the Change Style drop-down list in the Format toolbar.

■ **Insert line breaks:** Use the Enter or Shift+Enter keys to insert line breaks into your Web page. These keys operate a bit differently in FrontPage Express than in typical word processing programs.

In a word processing program, pressing Enter sends your cursor down to the next line without inserting a blank line space between paragraphs. FrontPage Express, however, automatically inserts that blank line space, like so:

```
This is the first line.

This is the second line.
```

This feature is handy for delineating paragraphs on a Web page without having to indent. But what if you don't want that blank line space? That's when you use Shift+Enter. Pressing Shift+Enter makes the two lines single-spaced, like this:

```
This is the first line.
This is the second line.
```

To practice using FrontPage Express to add text to your Web page, type a heading and a paragraph, format the text, and use special characters and line breaks to add a copyright notice and address information to the bottom of the page. Of course, you can use whatever text or formatting you like. In Figure 2-3, you see the sample Orchid Club Home Page after I

- typed a heading and a text paragraph

- chose Arial Black for the text

- italicized the word *Cattley*

- applied the Heading 1 format and enlarged and centered the heading

- inserted the special copyright character and used line breaks to create the copyright notice and sample address information you see near the bottom-left corner of the page

Figure 2-3: A first stab at the sample home page.

Viewing Your Page in a Web Browser

FrontPage Express gives you a pretty good view of how your Web page looks in a Web browser. However, not all Web browsers are created equal. For example, your page may look slightly different in Netscape Navigator than in Microsoft Internet Explorer. You can't do much about these differences; you just have to live with them. But if you have two or more Web browsers installed on your computer, you may want to take a peek at your page in each of them to see how things look.

At any given time, only one of your Web browsers is registered as the default Web browser. Typically, when you open the browser that's not set as the default, you see a message asking if you want to make that browser the default. If you choose Yes, that browser becomes the default until you open some other browser and then choose Yes to make that new one the default. You don't need to make the browser the default to view your Web page, however.

You can open your sample page in the default Web browser by using one of the following methods:

- Choose Start⇨Documents, and then click the name of the page you want to open. (If the page isn't listed in the Documents menu, the page has been replaced by more recent documents.)

- Open your C:\Inetpub\wwwroot folder (if you created a desktop shortcut to that folder, just click that shortcut icon). Then double-click the icon for the page you want to view.

When the page opens, keep in mind that it appears exactly as it would appear to someone on the Internet using the same kind of browser. You can't make changes to the page while in the Web browser. You can only view the page. To close the page, just close your Web browser.

To view your page in a browser other than your default browser, just start up that browser as you normally would. After the browser is open on your desktop, you need to change whatever is in the Address/Location bar to whatever Personal Web Server defined as your site's location. The syntax for that name is http://computername, where *computername* is the name of the computer on which the page is stored. In my case, the computer is named poweredge, so the URL of my home page is http://poweredge. After typing the correct URL for your site, press Enter, and the home page of your site appears within the browser.

Viewing Your Page's HTML

You really don't need to learn HTML because FrontPage Express automatically creates HTML for you as you create and edit your Web page. However, if you want to see the HTML that FrontPage Express creates, follow these steps:

1. Open the page in FrontPage Express.

2. Choose View⇨HTML from the FrontPage Express menu bar.

A new window titled View or Edit HTML appears, as shown in Figure 2-4. Seeing the page with all its HTML tags exposed, rather than hidden, is often called viewing the page's *source*. The HTML tags in the page's source are easy to see because the tags are always enclosed in angle brackets (<>). The tag name is shown in purple. Many HTML tags exist in pairs. One tag starts the format, and a similar tag with a slash in front of the tag name ends the format. For example, the title of a page is enclosed in <title>...</title> tags. The title of the sample page looks like this:

```
<title>Orchid Club Home Page</title>
```

Figure 2-4: A look at the sample page's HTML.

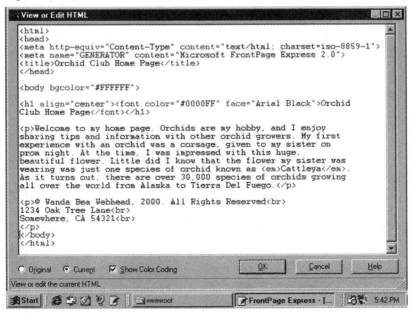

Some HTML tags use *attributes*, which further define the appearance of text within the tags. For example, the `<h1>...</h1>` tags surround any text that's formatted as a Heading 1. But if you look at the page headline for the sample page, you see something like this:

```
<h1 align="center">Orchid Club Home Page</h1>
```

The *align* attribute tells the `<h1>` tag how to align the heading. Attributes, such as *align*, are shown in red. The `=center"` part is the *value* assigned to the *align* attribute. Hence, the heading is centered.

I also changed the font and color of the sample page's headline. The `<font>...</font>` tags show how HTML applies the font. To the left of the headline is the tag that defines the font face and color; the tag looks like this:

```
<font color="#0000FF" face="Arial Black">
```

At the end of the text is the `</font>` tag that terminates that font format.

You may wonder about the `color ="#0000FF"` attribute and value. HTML uses a *hex triplet* (also called an *rgb triplet*) to define a color. The # symbol simply tells HTML that the number that follows is a triplet. The first pair of digits represents the amount of red, the second pair represents the amount of green, and the third pair represents the amount of blue required to show the color. Each pair of numbers can range from 00 to FF, where FF is the number 255 converted to a hexadecimal number.

Fortunately, you don't have to worry about hex triplets or hexadecimal numbers when defining colors in your Web pages, because you can create colors using the Color dialog box, as you do in a word processing program.

You can actually make changes and corrections to your page in the View or Edit HTML window. However, I don't recommend messing with your page's HTML tags until you know more about HTML in general. For the moment, just click OK near the bottom of the View or Edit HTML window and get back to formatting your page in FrontPage Express.

You can view the source of any Web page you visit using your Web browser. In Microsoft Internet Explorer, choose View⇨Source from the menu bar. In Netscape Navigator, choose View⇨Page Source.

Hopefully, this chapter seems pretty easy to you, and you're whizzing through entering and formatting text on your Web page. Things get a bit more complicated as you progress, but the basic skills for entering, editing, and formatting text apply to a lot of your work. After all, you're bound to put text in your Web pages! In the next chapter, you learn how to reopen this page for further editing, and you discover more advanced techniques for formatting your text.

CHAPTER 3
ADDING LINES, LISTS, AND OTHER GOODIES

IN THIS CHAPTER

- Reopening your page for editing
- Adding horizontal bars
- Applying the predefined Address format
- Typing lists
- Indenting and spacing text

In this chapter, you reopen your page in FrontPage Express. You find out how to add separator lines, use the Address format, type different kinds of lists, and indent and space text. You may not use all these features in your sample Web page, but you do use enough of them to give you some hands-on experience that you can use to create pages on your own.

Reopening Your Page in FrontPage Express

If you want to reopen your page to make changes or corrections, start FrontPage Express. Initially, you're faced with a blank page. To reopen a recently edited page, open the File menu and look near the bottom for the name of the page you want to open. Click that name, and the page appears, ready for editing.

If the page you want to edit is no longer available from the File menu, choose File⇨Open. Use the Browse button to browse to your C:\Inetpub\wwwroot folder and then double-click the name of the page you want to open.

If most of the time you use Microsoft Internet Explorer Version 5 as your Web browser, you can get the best of both worlds. While viewing your page via Internet Explorer, choose File⇨Edit with Microsoft FrontPage Editor from the Internet Explorer menu bar. A second copy of your page opens, this time in FrontPage Express.

Be aware that even though the page is open at that moment in both Internet Explorer and FrontPage Express, changes you make in FrontPage Express don't immediately carry over to Internet Explorer. If you want to see recent changes in the Web browser, you first need to save the current version of the page by clicking the Save button in the FrontPage Express toolbar. Then click the Refresh button in the Internet Explorer toolbar.

Adding Separator Lines

You can use separator lines (also called *horizontal rules*) in Web pages to separate chunks of text. For example, the sample page needs a separator line above the copyright information that you added in the previous chapter. Adding a separator line in FrontPage Express is easy. Just follow these steps:

1. Click where you want the line to appear. If you need to add a blank line between two lines to make room, move the cursor to the end of the upper line and press the Enter key.

2. Choose Insert⇨Horizontal Line from the FrontPage Express menu bar.

The line stretches the width of the page. If you end up with too much blank space above or below the line, try moving the cursor to the blank line and pressing the Delete key. If you inadvertently delete the line, you can bring it back by choosing Edit⇨Undo Clear.

The gray line that initially appears in your page is just the *default* horizontal line. Unless you specify otherwise, Front-Page Express assumes that you want a gray line that's the width of the page. As with many formatting features, you can change the line by changing its properties. Here's how:

1. Right-click the line that you want to change.

2. Choose Horizontal Line Properties from the menu that appears.

The Horizontal Line Properties dialog box appears. Within it, you can specify the width of the line, either in points or as a percentage of the width of the page. You can change the line's height (thickness), alignment, and color. You can also choose the line's display as either a solid or shaded line. Make your selections from the dialog box and then click OK.

If ever you're wondering how to change some formatted item in your page, try right-clicking the item to see if an option for changing the item's properties appears on the menu that pops up. No harm in trying!

Using the Address Format

In the Change Style drop-down list mentioned in Chapter 2, you may notice a format named Address. This format is typically used at the bottom of a page to show the name and address and/or copyright information of the Web site's owner. No rule says that you must use the Address format to style such text — doing so is just something of a convention. In most Web browsers, the formatted text simply looks italicized.

You can apply the Address format as you do any other. Select the text to which you want to apply the format and then choose the format from the Change Style drop-down list.

For example, after I selected the three lines of text at the bottom of the sample page and chose Address from the Change Style drop-down list, those lines appear in italics, as shown in Figure 3-1. As you see in that figure, I also inserted a horizontal rule between the body text and the copyright notice. I made the line 1 pixel tall and solid, which is why the line looks so thin. And although you can't tell in the figure, I made the line blue to match the color of the page's headline.

Figure 3-1:   Address format and horizontal rule added to the sample home page.

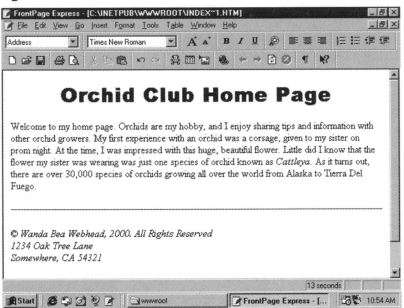

In case you're wondering, the HTML tag for displaying a horizontal rule is `<hr>`. The tags for displaying text in Address format are `<address>...</address>`.

Typing Lists

You can use lists as design elements in all forms of text. The two main types of lists are bulleted lists and numbered lists. For example, in this book, I often use bulleted lists to show a set of options. I use numbered lists to display step-by-step instructions. Lists are useful because they break large paragraphs of text into smaller, easier-to-read chunks of information.

The general technique for creating a list in FrontPage Express is to first type each item in the list. Press Enter after each item. Don't type any numbers or special characters in front of each item. After you type the list, select it. Then apply one of the list styles to the selection. List styles are available on the toolbar as well as in the Change Style drop-down list. In Figure 3-2, you can see the small bulleted list that I added to the sample home page. I also put in the "Places to Go" heading, formatted as a Heading 2 and displayed in Arial font.

To create the list, move the cursor to the end of the new heading and press Enter to insert a new line. Then click the Bulleted List button in the toolbar. Type **Common Orchids,** press Enter, type **Cool Orchid Sites,** and again press Enter. Then click the Bulleted List button to end the list.

Because I thought the text in the list looked a little small, I also increased its size by selecting the text and using the Text Size button in the toolbar.

Figure 3-2: A new heading and bulleted list added to the sample page.

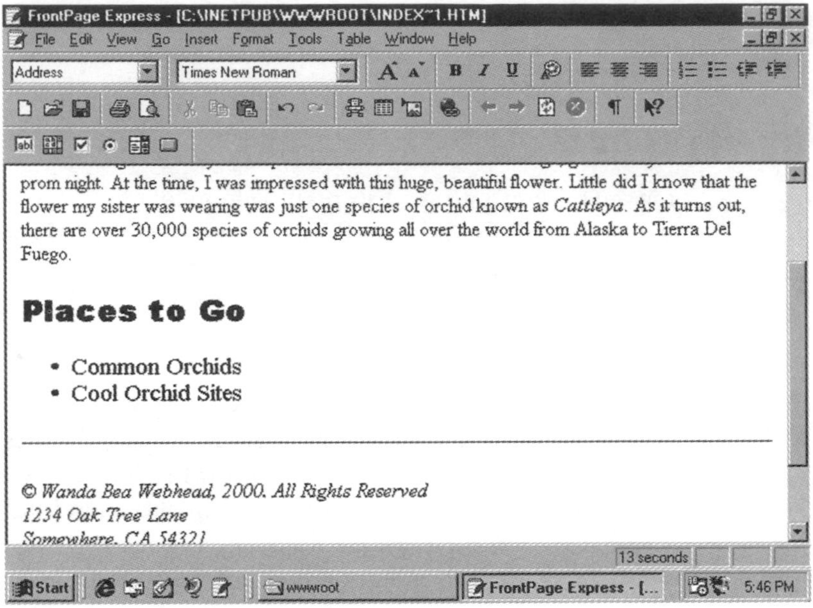

prom night. At the time, I was impressed with this huge, beautiful flower. Little did I know that the flower my sister was wearing was just one species of orchid known as *Cattleya*. As it turns out, there are over 30,000 species of orchids growing all over the world from Alaska to Tierra Del Fuego.

Places to Go

- Common Orchids
- Cool Orchid Sites

© *Wanda Bea Webhead, 2000. All Rights Reserved*
1234 Oak Tree Lane
Somewhere, CA 54321

Fixing list problems

When you're first figuring out how to create lists, you're bound to make a few mistakes. Here are some easy fixes for common errors in lists:

■ To remove a dangling bullet or number with no text after it, move the cursor just to the right of that bullet or number and press Backspace to delete it.

■ To make a number or bullet appear and disappear, place the cursor anywhere in the list item and click the Numbered List or Bulleted List button in the toolbar.

■ To add blank space between items in a bulleted list, move the cursor to the end of the top line and press Enter to add a blank line. Then click the Bulleted List button in the toolbar to hide the bullet. Press Delete if you want to narrow the space between the lines.

Some of the formatting techniques described in the next section, as well as the discussion on indenting and outdenting that follows, can help you gain control over your lists.

Formatting lists

You can change the default list that appears when you apply the Numbered List or Bulleted List format to a list of items. In fact, you can easily change one type of list to the other. To format a list, follow these steps:

1. Right-click any item in the list.

2. Choose List Properties from the menu that appears near the mouse pointer. The List Properties dialog box appears, as shown in Figure 3-3. You can choose any of three different bullet styles (or no bullet) on the Bulleted tab. The Numbered tab enables you to choose any of six different numbering styles. On the Numbered tab, you can also choose the starting number or letter for the list. The Other tab enables you to choose from among five different list styles, which I discuss later in this chapter.

3. After making your selection(s) from the dialog box, click OK. The program applies your selection(s) to the list as a whole, and the dialog box closes.

You can also change the properties of a single item in the list. Just right-click the list item you want to change and choose List Item Properties from the menu that appears.

Figure 3-3: The List Properties dialog box.

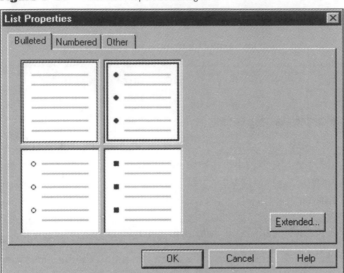

Ignoring menu and directory lists

When viewing options in the Change Style drop-down list, you may notice two additional list styles, named Menu List and Directory List. Oddly enough, the vast majority of Web browsers display bulleted lists, menu lists, and directory lists in the same manner. So you have no reason to use a menu list or directory list rather than a bulleted list. Strange but true.

Using definition lists

Another type of list is called the *definition list.* Use this type of list for a glossary or similar list that presents some word or phrase followed by its definition. The definition list actually involves two styles, one named Defined Term, for the term being defined, and a second style named Definition that formats the definition you type.

To type a definition list, follow these steps:

1. Type the term to be defined and then choose Defined Term from the Change Style drop-down list.

2. Press Enter and type the term's definition. (FrontPage Express automatically applies the Definition style to the text.)

3. Press Enter and then type the next term to be defined. (FrontPage Express automatically applies the Defined Term style to the text you type.)

4. Repeat Steps 2 and 3 until you finish typing all the items in your list.

If you make any mistakes, you can always go back and select any chunk of text and reapply the Defined Term or Definition style to that text. If you want to add an extra blank line between defined terms, move the cursor to the left of any defined term in the list and then press Enter.

If you need to neatly align text into two or more columns, your best bet is to use tables, which I discuss in Chapter 6.

Indenting Text

You can easily indent text from the left and right margins. In paragraphs, you can use these indentations to display lengthy quotations (called *block quotes*) like the one you see in the second paragraph in Figure 3-4. You can also indent list items, such as the two bulleted items in the list shown in Figure 3-4.

Figure 3-4: Examples of an indented paragraph and list items.

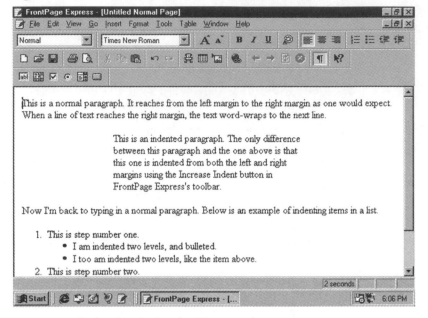

Indenting is simple. Here are the steps:

1. Click anywhere within the paragraph that you want to indent. To indent multiple paragraphs or list items, first select them.

2. Click the Increase Indent or Decrease Indent button in the toolbar until the level of indentation looks good to you.

If you try to indent a line of text in FrontPage Express by pressing the spacebar, you may be surprised to find that you can't insert blank spaces that way. FrontPage Express just ignores the spacebar. You can, however, precisely indent a line of text, as you find out in the next section.

Using Preformatted and Monospaced Text

HTML and Web browsers normally use proportional fonts to display text. A *proportional font* is one in which different letters are different widths, and blank spaces can be adjusted to best fit text on the line. The downside to proportional fonts is that they make it impossible to indent text using blank spaces. To get really tight control over the exact placement of characters in a chunk of text, you need to use a *monospace font*, in which each character, including each blank space, is exactly the same width. However, choosing a specific font in HTML is risky, because you can never be sure the visitor's computer has the exact font you select.

For this reason, HTML provides a *Formatted* style (also called the *Preformatted* style) that automatically uses whatever monospace font is available on the visitor's computer. After you apply the Formatted style to a section of your Web page, you automatically switch to a monospace font and can use blank spaces to control the level of indentation of each item of text.

Figure 3-5 shows a couple of examples. In the first example, below the first body paragraph, I used the Formatted style to print some information about a hypothetical book. I was able to line up text to the left and right of the colons by using simple blank spaces. The second example illustrates another common use of the Formatted style — to show an example of code written in a programming language.

Using the Formatted style is easy. Just follow these steps:

1. Place the cursor at the line where you plan to start typing the formatted text.

2. Choose Formatted from the Change Style drop-down list.

3. Type your text as you usually do.

4. When you want to change back to the proportional font, press Enter to end the last line of formatted text. Then choose Normal from the Change Style drop-down list.

Figure 3-5: Two examples of Formatted text.

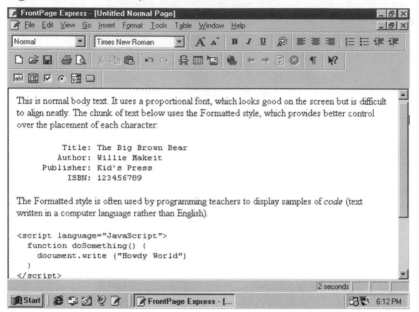

When you type formatted text, you can type as you usually do. About the only difference you discover while typing in the Formatted style is that you can press the spacebar to insert as many spaces as you want at the beginning of the line or between words. Also, lengthy lines don't automatically wrap to the next line when you type past the edge of the screen.

To convert regular text to Formatted text, select the text you want to convert and choose Formatted from the Change Style drop-down list. To convert Formatted text back to normal body text, select the text and choose Normal from the Change Style drop-down list.

Formatting and Beyond

The techniques you discover in this chapter can make it easy for you to format your text to your liking. The procedure is really quite simple. Type some text, select it, and then choose a Style from the Change Style drop-down list in the toolbar or click the appropriate button in the toolbar. After you apply a style, you can change or tweak it by right-clicking the formatted text and choosing the appropriate Properties option from the menu that appears.

In the next chapter, you discover another way to embellish your Web pages — by adding graphic images. As you see, Front-Page Express makes it easy to add a picture to your page, to size and position the picture, and even to wrap text around it.

CHAPTER 4
ADDING GRAPHICS AND MULTIMEDIA

IN THIS CHAPTER

- Understanding graphic file types

- Adding a picture to your page

- Wrapping text around a picture

- Adding wallpaper

- Adding background music

A Web page consisting of only text would be boring. Color, pictures, and sound are what really bring a Web page to life. In this chapter, you discover how to add pictures to your Web page. You find out how to color or wallpaper your page's background. You also learn to add background music or a sound effect to your page.

Understanding Graphic Images

Graphic images stored on computer disks come in many *file formats*. The file format describes how the information in the file gets converted to a picture. The majority of Web browsers on the Internet support only two of those formats, commonly known as GIF and JPEG formats. GIF is short for the CompuServe Graphics Interchange Format. The GIF format is generally used for cartoons, illustrations, line drawings, and such, because it supports only 256 colors. However, one of those colors may be transparent, which enables you to create images with transparent backgrounds.

The other file format, supported by virtually all Web browsers, was created by the Joint Photographic Experts Group, hence the filename extension JPEG or JPG. This file format supports millions of colors and is therefore much better suited for transporting photographs than the GIF format. However, because this format is primarily used for photos, no support for transparency exists in JPEG files.

Where to find graphic images

If you're an artist, or at least semi-competent at using a graphics program, you can create your own graphic images using just about any graphics program on the market. However, if you're new to all of this, you may want to use existing images in your Web site. Several resources are available to you for finding ready-made images, including the following:

- **Clip art collections:** You can purchase clip art collections containing thousands of images at any computer store.

- **Web sites:** Some Web sites offer free Web art. To start your search, check out www.coolnerds.com/webart and the links at www.coolnerds.com/webart/graflinx.htm. The Clip Art Archives at www.onlinebusiness.com/shops/_clipart/BEST_OF_WEB_clipart.shtml also provide links to lots of graphic images.

- **Photographs:** If you have favorite photos, you can scan them into digital pictures for use on the Web. If you don't have a scanner, many copy services now offer scanning as a service.

If you need a custom logo, most cities have businesses that create custom logos and related artwork. Check your Yellow Pages under Graphic Designers. If you go with such a service, make sure you tell them that you plan to use the logo on the Web, so that they can deliver the artwork to you in an appropriate format.

Much of the material on the Internet is copyrighted, which means you can't use it without permission from the copyright holder. If a Web site doesn't specifically state that the images are freely available for use, be sure to check with the owner of the image before using the image in your Web site.

Changing and converting graphic images

If you purchase a clip art collection, the images in that collection may not be in the JPEG or GIF format that you need. Furthermore, you may want to resize an image, crop it, or change it in some other way. To do these things, you need a graphics manipulation program and some time to learn how to use it. Even though this book doesn't get into manipulating graphics in any great depth, I can recommend a product that you may want to download and try risk-free. The product is called Paint Shop Pro 5, and you can download a trial version of it from www.jasc.com. If you use the trial version, you're on your own in terms of figuring out how things work. If you purchase the real version, you receive a printed manual that can help you learn the ropes a lot more quickly.

Paint Shop Pro 5 also includes the features you need to create transparent-background GIF images.

One of the beauties of Paint Shop Pro is that you can open an image in just about any format conceivable. Afterward, you can convert the image to GIF or JPEG by simply choosing File⇨Save As from the Paint Shop Pro menu bar. In the dialog box that appears, choose CompuServe Graphics Interchange (*.gif) or JPEG — JFIF Compliant (*.jpg, *.jif, *.jpeg) from the Save as Type drop-down list. Give the image a filename, and you're done. You have an Internet-ready JPEG or GIF image to put on your Web page.

Getting images to the right folder

You want to keep in mind that even though your picture appears as part of your page, the picture is actually stored in a file separate from the page. Also, that picture must exist in its own file on your Web server so that visitors download the image when they load your page into their browsers.

To minimize the likelihood of forgetting to upload your pictures, copy (or move) the graphic image into your C:\Inetpub\wwwroot folder before you add the image to your page. That way, when you upload your pages to your Web site, all the files that you need to upload are right there in one folder.

If you create a desktop shortcut to the C:\Inetpub\wwwroot folder, as I suggest in Chapter 1, you can move the image into that folder by simply dragging the image onto the desktop shortcut. Or you can use whatever Windows technique for moving and copying files that you prefer.

Inserting a Picture into Your Page

Inserting a picture into your Web page is easy. Here's how:

1. Click to bring the cursor to the spot in your page where you want to place the upper-left corner of the picture.

2. Click the Insert Image button in the toolbar or choose Insert➪Image from the FrontPage Express menu bar.

3. In the dialog box that appears, use the Browse button to get to the folder that contains the graphic image. If you moved the image to your C:\Inetpub\wwwroot folder, as suggested previously, browse to that folder.

4. Double-click the name of the image you want to insert.

Don't be surprised if the image doesn't turn out quite the way you intend. For example, Figure 4-1 shows how the sample page looks immediately after I inserted a sample GIF file that I found. I prefer that the picture appear next to the text, not above it. So I have a little formatting to do.

Figure 4-1: The sample home page after first inserting a picture.

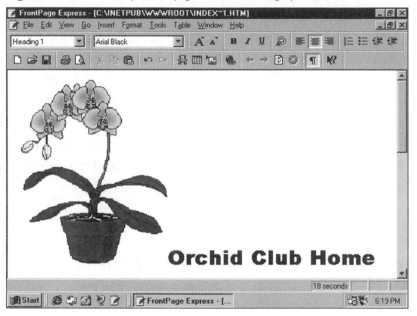

Wrapping text around a picture

You have several ways to handle a picture after placing it in your page. The simplest way is to alter the picture's properties. Here's how:

1. Right-click the picture you want to change.

2. Choose Image Properties from the menu that appears. The Image Properties dialog box appears.

At this juncture, you're mainly concerned with the options on the Appearance tab. The first option, Alignment, enables you to decide how you want to place the picture in relation to nearby text. When placing a fairly large picture in your document, you probably want to choose from among the following options:

- **Bottom:** One paragraph of text aligns next to the bottom of the picture (refer to Figure 4-1).

- **Middle:** One paragraph of text aligns next to the middle of the picture.

- **Top:** One paragraph of text aligns next to the top of the picture.

- **Left:** The picture appears to the left of all neighboring text.

- **Right:** The picture appears to the right of all neighboring text.

As you see in Figure 4-2, choosing the Left alignment option for the picture places it at the left side of the page and wraps all the neighboring text around the picture.

Sizing and spacing pictures

You can also size and format your picture using the following other options on the Appearance tab of the Image Properties dialog box:

- **Border Thickness:** Indicates in pixels the thickness of the border around the image. A setting of 0 indicates no border.

- **Horizontal Spacing:** Sets the spacing between the picture and text that wraps to the left or right of the picture.

- **Vertical Spacing:** Sets the spacing between the picture and text that wraps above or below the picture.

- **Specify Size:** Allows you to specify how wide and how tall you want the picture to be.

Figure 4-2: The sample home page after aligning the picture to the left of neighboring text.

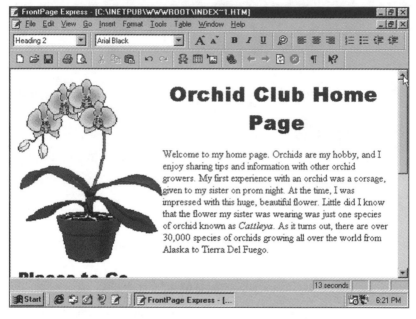

- **Width:** Defines the width of the picture in pixels or as a percent of the original width.

- **Height:** Defines the height of the picture in pixels or as a percent of the original height.

If you can't get the size right using the Width and Height options, close the dialog box and return to your document. Click your picture to make sure that it's selected. You see sizing handles (little squares) around the picture. You can change the size of your picture by dragging any of those sizing handles. To avoid changing the proportions of the picture, drag a corner handle rather than one of the handles on the side of the picture.

Alternate text

Some pictures, especially large photos, take a while to get across the Internet to visitors' browsers. To make the wait more bearable for your visitors, you can simply add a textual description of the picture to the page. These textual descriptions are also called *alternate text*. The alternate text appears pretty rapidly on visitors' screens, so they have at least some idea of what's coming, even though they can't see the picture. Visitors can also stop loading the page if they know from the alternate text description that they don't want or need to see the image. In addition, some Web browsers can't show graphic images, so the browsers show the image's alternate text instead.

You can create your own alternate text for any image in your page. To do so, right-click the image, choose Image Properties, and click the General tab of the Image Properties dialog box. Type the image's alternate text as the Text option. For example, in Figure 4-3 "Picture of orchid" is the alternative text for the orchid01.gif image.

Forcing text below a picture

When wrapping text around a picture, you may run into a situation in which you want to force a paragraph or heading to appear below the picture, rather than next to the picture. Fortunately, you can easily do so by following these steps:

1. Move the cursor to where you want the text to stop wrapping next to the picture.

Figure 4-3: The General tab of the Image Properties dialog box.

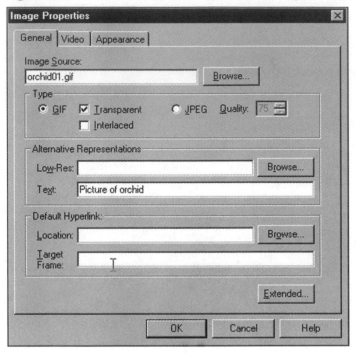

2. Choose Insert⇨Break from the FrontPage Express menu bar. The Break Properties dialog box appears.

3. Choose Clear Both Margins.

4. Click OK. All text to the right of the cursor position begins below, rather than next to, the picture.

If images are to the left and right of the text, and you just want to break text under one of those images, choose Clear Left Margin or Clear Right Margin, rather than Clear Both Margins.

Using Inline Images

An *inline image* is a tiny graphic image that you can use to call attention to some line of text. Some people use tiny inline images as custom bullets in bulleted lists. Tiny words like *new* or *cool* are often used to point out particular chunks of text. You can find these tiny images in many Web sites or create your own after you know how to use some kind of graphics program. After you find or create such an image, don't forget to save a copy of it in your C:\Inetpub\wwwroot folder along with the other files that make up your Web site.

Tip

For some freebie examples of small inline images, see www.coolnerds.com/webart/bullets.htm and the Bullets, Buttons, Icons link at www.cool nerds.com/links/graflinx.htm. Gilbert's Icon Archive at www.west world.com/~ghyatt/icons also offers lots of small inline graphic images.

Inserting an inline image into your text is no different than inserting any other image. You simply place the cursor where you want the image to appear. Then click the Insert Image button or choose Insert⇨Image from the menu to open the picture you want to display at that spot.

After you place the image, you can use the alignment options illustrated in Figure 4-4 to align the image with neighboring text. Right-click the image, choose Image Properties, click the Appearance tab, and then select an option from the Alignment drop-down list.

These options align text in relation to the *baseline* of neighboring text. The baseline is an imaginary line that runs along the bottom of most of the text. If you think of writing on a lined piece of notebook paper, the line that you write on is the baseline.

Figure 4-4: Examples of inline images aligned with neighboring text.

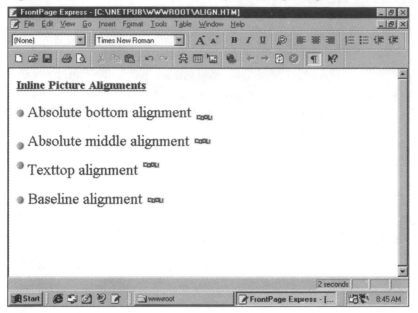

Some letters have *descenders*, pieces of the character that drop below the baseline. For example, the letters *g, j, p, q*, and *y* all have descenders because a part of the letter falls below the baseline. Some letters have *ascenders* that stick up higher than the tops of other lowercase letters. For example, the letters *b, d, f, h, k*, and *l* all have ascenders. Letters like *a, c, e, m*, and *n* are all the same height and have no ascenders or descenders. Here are descriptions of each type of image alignment:

- **absbottom:** Absolute bottom. Aligns the bottom of the image with the absolute bottom of the surrounding text. The absolute bottom is the baseline minus the height of the largest descender in the text.

- **absmiddle:** Absolute middle. Aligns the middle of the image with the middle of the surrounding text. The absolute middle is the midpoint between the absolute bottom and top of the surrounding text.

- **baseline:** Aligns the bottom of the image with the baseline of the text.

- **texttop:** Aligns the top of the image with the absolute top of the surrounding text. The absolute top is the baseline plus the height of the largest ascender in the text. Inline images are like any other image in that you can use all the options available in the Image Properties dialog box to format the picture. For example, you can use the Horizontal Spacing and Vertical Spacing options on the Appearance tab to add blank space around the image. Or use the Specify Size option on that same tab to size the picture.

The first time you save or close a Web page after adding a picture to the page, you may see a dialog box asking if you want to save the image to the current FrontPage web. Whenever you see this message, click Yes, which ensures that a copy of the picture is saved to the C:\Inetpub\wwwroot folder and makes sure that FrontPage Express "knows" that the picture is part of your overall Web site.

Changing Your Page's Background

The white background behind the text and pictures on your page need not be white. The background can be any color you like. Or you can use a graphic image as wallpaper for the background. The main trick to formatting the background of your page is to ensure that a good contrast exists between the background and the foreground. Otherwise, the text is difficult to read. For example, if you make your text white and your background yellow, the text is nearly impossible to read because you don't have enough contrast between the background and the letters. However, using dark blue letters against a yellow background provides plenty of contrast.

To change the color of your page's background and optionally the color of the text, follow these simple steps:

1. Choose Format⇨Background from the FrontPage Express menu bar.

2. Choose a color from the Background drop-down list.

3. (Optional) Choose a color from the Text drop-down list to change the color of the foreground text.

4. Click OK to apply your selections and close the dialog box.

Be aware that in your document some types of text, such as hyperlinks (see Chapter 5), are automatically colored differently from regular text. You want to keep this in mind when selecting a background color for your page.

If you want to use a picture as a background wallpaper, the first trick is to find a picture that works well as wallpaper. As a rule, you need an image that has very little contrast and is relatively pale, so that letters on the foreground contrast well with the image. You can find some sample background images to experiment with at `www.coolnerds.com/webart/bckframe.htm` and under Background Images at `www.coolnerds.com/links/graflinx.htm`.

After you find or create a background image that you like, be sure to copy or save it to your C:\Inetpub\wwwroot folder with the other files that make up your Web site.

In Figure 4-5, you see displayed in Paint Shop Pro an example picture of an orchid plant that I found in a clip art collection. Originally, the image had much more contrast. I used the Brightness and Contrast tools in Paint Shop Pro to tone down the image. (To get to those options in Paint Shop Pro, you choose Colors⇨Adjust⇨Brightness/Contrast.)

Figure 4-5:   An orchid picture I found and toned down using Paint Shop Pro.

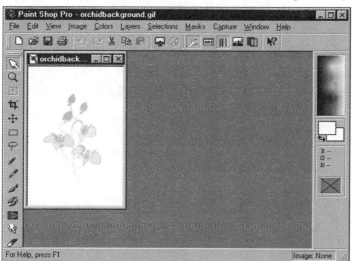

After you find or create a background image and save it in your C:\Inetpub\wwwroot folder, you can follow these simple steps to add the background image to your page:

1. In FrontPage Express, choose Format⇨Background.

2. Select the Background Image check box.

3. Use the Browse button to open your C:\Inetpub\wwwroot folder and select the name of the image that you want to use as your background wallpaper.

4. Click OK.

Figure 4-6 shows the sample page with the image from Figure 4-5 used as the background. Notice how the image is automatically tiled — in other words, the small image is repeated over and over again to fill in the page's entire background.

Figure 4-6: The faded orchid picture used as background in the sample home page.

As you scroll up and down a page, the background image scrolls up and down. You can lock the background so that it remains stationary as you scroll up and down through text. To do so, again choose Format⟹Background from the Front-Page Express menu bar. But this time, select the Watermark check box and then click OK.

If you choose both a background color and a background image, the background color can only show through the image if the background image is a GIF file with a transparent background.

Adding Background Sound

You can also have your page play a MIDI file or some sound effect when the page first opens in a visitor's browser. *MIDI* stands for *Musical Instrument Digital Interface*, and a MIDI file is one that contains music. If you're a musician who already knows how to create MIDI music, you can create your own custom MIDI files. However, if you're like most people, you probably want to search the Web for copyright-free MIDI files that you can use in your Web page. Just go to any search engine, such as www.yahoo.com, and search for "MIDI files" to see what you can find.

Most browsers also support *WAV* (wave) files. These files generally contain sound effects rather than music. You can find freebie WAV files on the Web by going to any search engine and searching for "wave files" or "WAV files." Typically, when you get to a site that offers free MIDI or WAV files, you can click a link to open (listen to) or save the file to disk. Usually, you just click the link, open the file, and then listen to it. If you want to use that sound effect in your page, click the same link again, but this time choose the Save option. When specifying where to save the file, specify your C:\Inetpub\wwwroot folder. If clicking a link doesn't give you the option to save the file to your own hard disk, right-click the link instead and choose Save Target As... from the menu that appears. Then save the file to your C:\Inetpub\wwwroot folder.

The MIDI file or sound effect plays only on computers that have sound capabilities. On other computers, the sound effect is generally just ignored.

To add the MIDI or sound file to your page, re-open your page in FrontPage Express. Then follow these steps:

1. Choose Insert⇨Background Sound from the FrontPage Express menu bar.

2. Click the Browse button and browse to your C:\Inetpub\wwwroot folder.

3. If you're adding a WAV file, choose WAV Sound (*.WAV) from the Files of Type drop-down list. If you're adding a MIDI file, choose MIDI Sequencer (*.mid) from that drop-down list.

4. Click the name of the background sound file and then click the Open button.

The sound won't play immediately. All you've done at this point is add an HTML tag to your page that allows the sound to be played. To actually hear the file, close your page and save it. Then open the page in Microsoft Internet Explorer.

Warning

Unfortunately, FrontPage Express adds the HTML required to play the sound in Microsoft Internet Explorer only. You can't hear the background sound in other browsers, such as Netscape Navigator. Getting a background sound to play in multiple Web browsers is a little tricky and not something you can accomplish within FrontPage Express. Instead, you need to work directly in the document source and manually add some HTML and JavaScript. *JavaScript* is a programming language for Web pages and is beyond the scope of this book.

On the bright side, you don't need to know everything about JavaScript just to get a background sound to play. You can find the appropriate JavaScript code, as well as instructions for using it, at `www.coolnerds.com/jscript/bgsound.htm`. No need to reinvent the wheel!

CHAPTER 5

ADDING HYPERLINKS TO YOUR PAGES

IN THIS CHAPTER

- Linking to other Web sites
- Linking to other pages in your own site
- Creating e-mail links
- Using pictures as links
- Linking to sections within a page

If you spend any time at all on the Web, you know that a *hyperlink* is any hot spot on a page that a visitor can click to go to some other page. Typically, the link is a little piece of underlined text. However, a graphic image can also act as a hyperlink. As you learn in this chapter, adding hyperlinks to your page is easy in FrontPage Express. In this chapter, I use the Orchid Club Web site to illustrate how you can create hyperlinks. If you're building the sample site as you read the text, I suggest that you create a new page for the site by following these steps:

1. Start FrontPage Express in the usual manner, as discussed in Chapter 1.

2. Type **Orchid Club Links** to serve as the page's headline.

3. Choose Heading 1 from the Change Style drop-down list.

4. Select the headline and use the Change Font, Text Color, and Center toolbar buttons to format the headline to your liking.

5. Click the Save button in the toolbar.

6. Title this page Orchid Club Links and save it as links.htm in your http://*computername* folder, as shown in Figure 5-1.

Figure 5-1: The new page, saved with the filename links.htm, can offer hyperlinks to other Web sites.

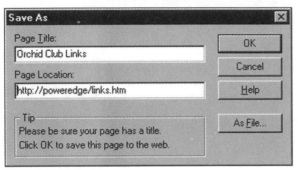

7. Click OK to save the page.

Now the Orchid Club Web site consists of two pages. The home page is saved under the filename index.html. The second page is saved under the filename links.htm. In this chapter, you can use the new links.htm page to learn how to create a hyperlink to an external Web site.

Linking to Other Web Sites

The simplest way to create a hyperlink in your Web site is to first type some text for the hyperlink, as well as any other descriptive text that you feel is appropriate. Select the text that you plan to use as the actual hyperlink and click the Create or Edit Hyperlink button to convert the text to a link. A dialog box titled Create Hyperlink appears. Type the URL of the page you want to link to into the URL textbox of that dialog box. Or you can cut and paste a URL into the textbox, as discussed in the "Cutting and pasting URLs" section later in this chapter.

To demonstrate, I typed more text into the links.htm page, including one bulleted list item, as shown in Figure 5-2. I selected the text My First Orchid to serve as the hyperlink.

Figure 5-2:   The small chunk of selected text in links.htm becomes a hyperlink to another Web page.

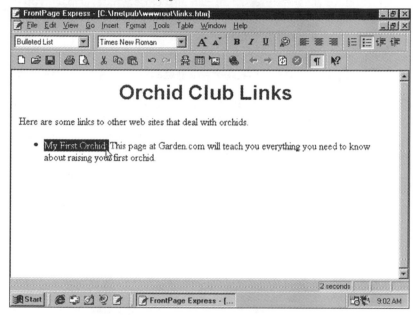

Testing a link in FrontPage Express

If you rest the mouse pointer on the hyperlink, the URL that the link points to appears in the FrontPage Express status bar near the lower-left corner of the screen. Clicking the hyperlink while you're working in FrontPage Express, however, doesn't take you to the other page. If you want to test the hyperlink in FrontPage Express, you need to hold down the Ctrl key and click the hyperlink.

If the link is valid, the page appears in FrontPage Express. To get back to the page you were editing, click the Back button in the FrontPage Express toolbar or choose Go⇨Back from the FrontPage Express menu bar. You can also choose a page to view and edit from the Window pull-down menu in FrontPage Express. You can also close whatever page you're viewing, without closing FrontPage Express, by choosing File⇨Close from the menu bar.

Cutting and pasting URLs

Sometimes when you're linking to a specific page in a large Web site, the URL to that page can be very lengthy. To avoid typing these lengthy URLs and possibly making mistakes, you can cut and paste the URL from your Web browser into your Web page. The procedure is simple; just follow these steps:

1. Start your Web browser and go to the page to which you want to create a link.

2. While viewing that page, click the page's URL in your Web browser's Address (or Location) bar to select the entire URL.

3. Press Ctrl+C or choose File⇨Copy to copy the URL onto the Windows clipboard. You won't see anything happen on the screen, but rest assured that a copy of the selected URL is on the clipboard.

4. Go back to the World Wide Web tab of the Create or Edit Hyperlink dialog box where you normally type the URL to the page. If you previously created the hyperlink and just need to change the link's URL, you can right-click the hyperlink and choose Hyperlink Properties. Select any text that's already in the URL textbox (including the http:// that appears by default). Press Ctrl+V or choose File⇨Paste to replace that selected text with the URL that you previously copied.

5. After you copy the URL onto the clipboard, it stays there until you put something else on the clipboard. So if you haven't typed the hyperlink text yet, you can still do so. Then select that text and click the Create or Edit Hyperlink button to open the Create Hyperlink dialog box and paste the URL.

6. Click OK to save the change and close the dialog box. (To test the link in FrontPage Express, hold down the Ctrl key and click the link.)

You can put as many hyperlinks as you wish on a page. To change a hyperlink that you previously created, just right-click the link anywhere and choose Hyperlink Properties.

Linking to Pages in Your Own Site

You can also create links to pages within your own Web site by using roughly the same basic techniques that you use to link to external Web sites. The Orchid Club example site currently has two Web pages: the home page index.html and the new links.htm page. But the reader has no way to get from the home page to the links.htm page, so you need to create a link.

If you plan to add hyperlinks to a page you just created in FrontPage Express, be sure to save the page first. FrontPage Express must know where this page is in relation to other pages in your site in order to set up the links correctly.

Follow the steps below to create the link:

1. Open both the page you want to link to and the page you want to contain the link. In the example, you need to have both index.html and links.htm open. Use the File menu in FrontPage Express to open both pages. Normally, only one page at a time is visible on the screen. But you can flip back and forth between the open pages by opening the Window pull-down menu in FrontPage Express and clicking the name of the page you want to bring to the forefront. In this example, you want to place the link in index.html, so that page needs to be visible in FrontPage Express.

2. When you have two or more pages open in FrontPage Express, you can use the Cascade and Tile options on the Window menu to view portions of multiple pages simultaneously.

3. Select the text that you plan to use as the hyperlink. In the example, I selected the text Cool Orchid Sites.

4. Click the Create or Edit Hyperlink button or choose Insert↪Hyperlink from the FrontPage Express menu bar. The Create Hyperlink dialog box appears. Because the example page you plan to link to is already open, click the Open Pages tab. The dialog box shows the titles of all open pages. Here, you want to link to the Orchid Club Links page, so click that page title. I selected the Cool Orchid Sites text near the bottom of index.html and, as shown in Figure 5-3, selected Orchid Club Links as the page to link to.

5. Click OK. A warning about linking to a local file may appear. You can ignore the warning by clicking the Yes button. As long as you upload the page to your Web server, when the time comes, you won't have a problem.

After the dialog box closes, the selected text appears blue and underlined, like most links. When you point to the link, the name of the page that the link points to, in this example links.htm, appears in the status bar. To test the link, hold down the Ctrl key and click the link. You should arrive at links.htm. To return to index.html, click the Back button in the FrontPage Express toolbar.

Figure 5-3: Selected text in index.html becomes a link to links.htm.

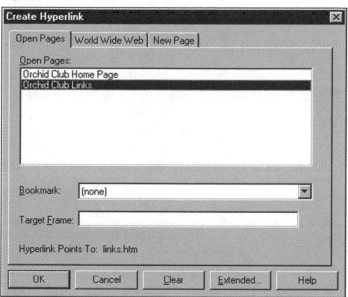

When you create a link to a page within your own Web site and in the same directory as the page that contains the link, you don't need to use the entire URL. Just the page's filename, links.htm in this example, is sufficient.

Creating a Link to a New Page

FrontPage Express also enables you to create a new page and a link to that new page in one fell swoop. This feature is handy because you can set up your links while viewing the page that contains those links, and you can make up the page titles and filenames as you go along. The steps are nearly identical to creating a link to an existing page within your site. To try this feature, you can follow the steps below to create a link in your home page to a nonexistent page named commonorchids.htm:

1. Type and then select the text that you want to serve as the hyperlink — Common Orchids in the example.

2. Click the Create or Edit Hyperlink button or choose Insert⟫Hyperlink from the menu bar.

3. In the Create Hyperlink dialog box that appears, click the New Page tab. The dialog box suggests a title and filename for this new page. You can use the suggested text or create your own. In Figure 5-4, you can see that I selected the text that I want to serve as the hyperlink. And you can see that I titled the new page and named it commonorchids.htm.

Figure 5-4: Create a hyperlink and new page in one fell swoop.

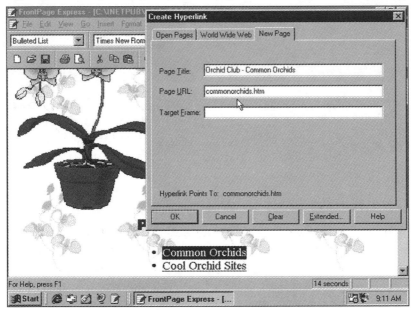

4. Click OK, and you see a New Page dialog box that enables you to select a wizard or template for this new page.

5. Select Normal Page and then click OK. The new, blank page fills the screen. You don't need to create the entire

page just yet. In fact, I suggest that you type only the page headline, **Common Orchids**. You can format the text as a Heading 1, center it, and do whatever else you want.

6. Select File⇨Save As from the FrontPage Express menu bar to save the new page.

7. When the Save As dialog box appears, make sure the Page Location box specifies your http://*computername* directory. And make sure the filename matches what you specified when creating the link. (In the example, I need to make sure that this new page is saved as http://poweredge/commonorchids.htm.)

8. Click OK.

To see your new hyperlink, go back to the index.html page (or whichever page you put the hyperlink in) by clicking the Back button in the toolbar or by selecting the page from the Window menu on the menu bar. As usual, pointing to the link shows the name of the page (in the example, commonorchids.htm) in the status bar. To test the link, hold down the Ctrl key and click the link.

Because you have at least two of your Web pages open, you want to be sure to close and save everything. To do so, choose File⇨Close from the FrontPage Express menu bar. If the page has changed since you last saved it, a prompt asks whether you want to save those changes. Be sure to choose Yes. You can just keep choosing File⇨Close and then Yes to close and save your pages, until you have no pages visible in FrontPage Express.

To verify that all your Web site's files are in your C:\Inetpub\wwwroot folder, you can open that folder using My Computer or Windows Explorer. (If you set up a shortcut to that folder, just click the shortcut on your Windows desktop.) The folder should contain the Web pages you previously created (index.html, links.htm, and commonorchids.htm in the example). Also, the folder should contain a file for each graphic image you previously added to your pages (orchid01.gif and orchidbackground.gif in the example). If you added a background sound file to your site, that file should also appear in the C:\Inetpub\wwwroot folder.

Your C:\Inetpub\wwwroot folder contains folders named _private, cgi-bin, and images and may contain files named vti_inf.html, default.asp, global.asa, and postinfo.html. Don't worry about these files, but don't delete them. FrontPage Express needs these folders and files to do its job.

Creating E-mail Links

You can add to any page in your site a link to your own e-mail address. When a visitor clicks that link, his or her e-mail program opens and displays an empty e-mail form that's pre-addressed with your e-mail address. The visitor just needs to type in a message and click his or her Send button to send you the message. Creating an e-mail link is virtually identical to creating any other kind of link. Here are the exact steps:

1. In FrontPage Express, open the page in which you want to place the e-mail link.

2. Move the cursor to where you want the link to appear and type the link text (e.g., **Contact Me** or **E-mail Me**).

3. Select the text that you just typed.

4. Click the Create or Edit Hyperlink button in the toolbar or choose Insert⇨Hyperlink from the menu bar. The Create Hyperlink dialog box appears.

5. In the World Wide Web tab, choose mailto: from the Hyperlink Type drop-down list.

6. Type your e-mail address next to the mailto: chunk of text in the URL textbox. For example, in Figure 5-5 you can see that I typed and selected the words **Contact Me** near the bottom of the page and then set up the e-mail link to my e-mail address as `alan@coolnerds.com`.

7. Click OK.

Figure 5-5:   An e-mail hyperlink to my e-mail address at `alan@coolnerds.com`.

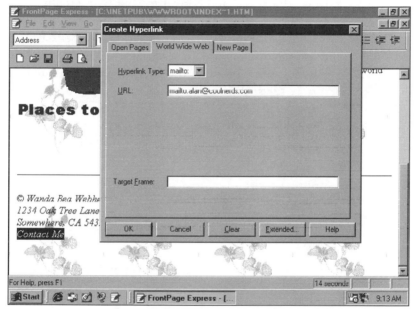

As usual, you can then click anywhere in your Web page to deselect the selected text. Pointing to the new hyperlink reveals the underlying URL in the status bar, which is mailto: followed by your e-mail address. Unfortunately, you can't test this type of link in FrontPage Express. But you can certainly test the link in your Web browser. Just close and save the page and then open it in any Web browser of your choosing. Click the e-mail link, and your e-mail program should open with a form addressed to you. Fill in the subject, type a message to yourself, and click the Send button.

Using Graphic Images as Links

No rule says that a hyperlink has to be text. You can use any graphic image as a link. The procedure is virtually identical to setting up a regular textual hyperlink. First, you need to find a graphic image and copy it to your C:\Inetpub\wwwroot folder, as usual. Then you need to place in your page the graphic image that you want to use as the link. (See Chapter 4 for information on how to place a graphic image in your Web page.) After you place the image in your page, follow these steps to use the image as a hyperlink:

1. Double-click the image or right-click the image and choose Image Properties from the menu that appears.

2. Under Default Hyperlink, click the Browse button next to the Location textbox. The Create Hyperlink dialog box appears.

3. Create your link by using any of the techniques described earlier in this chapter.

4. Click OK to close the Create Hyperlink dialog box.

5. Click OK to close the Image Properties dialog box.

You return to your Web page, and the graphic image remains selected. You need to click outside the picture to deselect it. Then when you point to the picture, you see the link's URL in the status bar. As usual, to test the link, hold down the Ctrl key and click the picture (unless it's an e-mail link, in which case you need to test it via your Web browser).

Nothing about the graphic image makes it obvious that it's a link. When visitors come to your site, the only way they know that a graphic is a hyperlink is by pointing to it. Whenever the mouse pointer touches a clickable hot spot, the pointer changes to a little hand with the index finger raised.

If you want to make a graphic image stand out more as a link, you can put a blue border around it. While not a common practice, it's an option. To place the blue border around the graphic image, you just need to add a normal border. (The fact that the image is a link automatically makes the border blue.) To add the border, go back to the Image Properties dialog box by double-clicking the image or by right-clicking the image and choosing Image Properties. On the Appearance tab, change the Border Thickness option to 1 or some higher number. Then click OK to close the dialog box.

Making Links to Page Sections

In a lengthy page, you may want to create links to sections within the same page. The Orchid Club example doesn't really have any such lengthy pages to use as an example, so I use a page from my Web site at www.coolnerds.com as an example. The page, which you can view at www.coolnerds.com/links/graflinx.htm, contains many links to sites offering Web graphics. The links are categorized into six different groups called Animated GIFs, Background Images, and so forth, as you can see near the top of Figure 5-6. Clicking one of those links takes you to the appropriate category within that same page.

To create a link within a page, you first need to define the *target*. The target is simply the place where the cursor lands when the reader clicks the link that leads to that spot. (The target is also called a *bookmark*.) The target can be a chunk of text, a picture, or even just some empty spot on the page. To create the target, follow these steps:

Figure 5-6: The links near the top of the page actually take the visitor to another section within the same page.

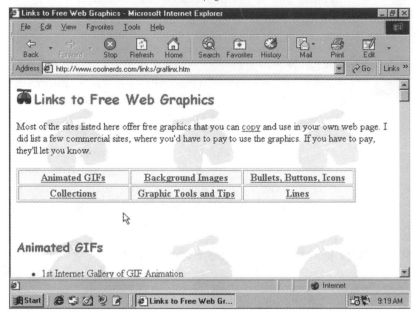

1. Move the cursor to the spot where you want the link to take the reader within the page.

2. (Optional) Select text or a graphic at that spot, if you like.

3. Choose Edit⇨Bookmark from the FrontPage Express menu bar.

4. Type any name you want for this bookmark. If you want the page to contain several bookmarks, make sure each has a unique name.

5. Click OK. A small flag icon appears at the cursor position. (This icon is visible only in FrontPage Express. The icon won't be visible in any Web browser.)

After you create a target, you can create a link to that target from anywhere within your page. Typically, you put the link near the top of the page, so the link is visible when the reader first views the page. Just move the cursor to where you want to place the link and type the link's text. Or if you plan to use a graphic image as the link, insert the graphic image at the spot.

You create the link to the target in much the same way as you create other links. Here are the exact steps:

1. Select the text or picture that you want to act as the hyperlink.

2. Click the Create or Edit Hyperlink button in the toolbar or choose Insert⇨Hyperlink from the menu bar. The Create Hyperlink dialog box appears.

3. Click the Open Page tab.

4. Make sure that the current page's title is selected under Open Pages.

5. Click the button to the right of the Bookmark drop-down list. The names of all the bookmarks in the current page appear. Click the name of the target that you want the link to point to.

6. Click OK to close the dialog box.

Back in your Web page, you can test the link in much the same way as you test other links. For example, if you deselect the link and then point to it, the status bar displays the target name preceded by a pound sign (#). The required pound sign tells the browser that the target is within the current page. To test the link, hold down the Ctrl key and click the link. FrontPage Express takes you to wherever you placed the target within the page.

That covers everything you need to know about hyperlinks. At this point, you know how to create all the major elements that make up a Web page — formatted text, graphic images, and hyperlinks. In the next chapter, you learn about tables, which give you a means of organizing text and graphics neatly into rows and columns on your pages.

CHAPTER 6

CREATING AND USING TABLES

- Creating a table
- Adding and coloring table borders
- Adding and deleting cells
- Merging and splitting cells
- Filling a table
- Formatting table cells

Tables are great tools for aligning text and pictures into neat rows and columns. Tables are entirely optional — no rule says that you must use tables in a given situation. However, you're bound to find them useful in any number of circumstances.

Creating a Table

A little terminology goes along with using tables, as pointed out in Figure 6-1.

- **Cell:** The blank space between lines within the table. A cell can contain text or a picture.
- **Column:** A vertical group of cells. The table in Figure 6-1 contains three columns.
- **Row:** A horizontal group of cells across the table. The table in Figure 6-1 contains five rows.

Figure 6-1: A sample table with various components labeled.

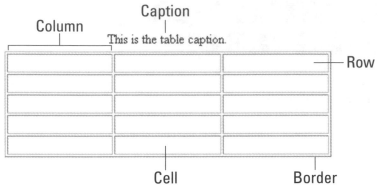

- **Border:** The lines that surround the table and each cell within the table.

- **Caption:** An optional line of text that describes the table.

You can gain fine control over the appearance and spacing of the table's parts. Specifically, you can control the appearance of the border, the *cell spacing* (the amount of space between each cell), and the *cell padding* (the margins used within the table). Figure 6-2 shows examples of a table with customized border, cell spacing, and cell padding. Note that the gray shades used in the figure identify different properties that you can adjust. They aren't shaded that way when you're working in FrontPage Express.

Figure 6-2: Borders, cell spacing, and cell padding are adjustable.

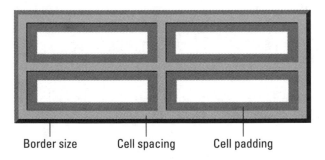

The steps for creating a table are simple. You can do so in one of two ways. If you want to create a quick table that uses the default widths and other settings, you can draw the table into your Web page by following these steps:

1. Open your page in FrontPage Express.

2. Move the cursor to the spot where you want the table to appear.

3. Click the Insert Table button in the toolbar. A grid appears beneath the button.

4. Drag the mouse pointer down and to the right through the grid to indicate the number of rows and columns you want in your table. Then release the mouse button.

5. The table appears with its upper-right corner located near the spot where you placed the cursor in Step 2.

The second way to create a table enables you to specify the number of rows and columns you desire and to set some values for the border thickness, cell spacing, and so forth. Getting all the settings just right the first time isn't imperative because you can change anything about your table at any time. But if you have in advance some idea of how you want to format the table, follow these steps:

1. Open your page in FrontPage Express.

2. Move the cursor to the spot where you want the table to appear.

3. Choose Table⇨Insert Table from the FrontPage Express menu bar. The Insert Table dialog box appears.

4. Specify the number of rows and columns you want your table to contain.

5. (Optional) Adjust any other settings that you wish to change in the dialog box.

6. Click OK.

The table appears in your page. If the border size is set to zero, no table borders are visible in the final page. However, FrontPage Express does show dotted lines as borders so that you can see the cells in the table. As you see in Figure 6-3, I inserted a table containing four rows and two columns into the commonorchids.htm page created in Chapter 5. If you want to follow along and create that same table, open your commonorchids.htm page in FrontPage Express. Then position the cursor below the page's main headline and insert a table of the same size using the technique I describe previously in the first set of steps. Leave the border size, cell spacing, cell padding, and other options at the default settings.

Figure 6-3: A table containing two columns and four rows in the commonorchids.htm page.

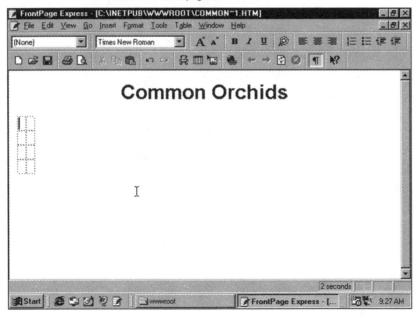

The dotted lines that identify the table borders are visible only if you click the Show/Hide (¶) button on the toolbar. When you deselect the button, the cell and table borders become invisible.

Sizing a table

You can size a table in either of two ways. One way is to simply let it size itself automatically as you add text and pictures to the table's cells. The second way is to specify your table's width, either in pixels or as a percentage of the width of the page. To give the table a predefined size, follow these steps:

1. Right-click anywhere within the table you want to size and choose Table Properties from the shortcut menu.

2. Under Minimum Width, select the Specify Width option.

3. Choose either *in Pixels* or *in Percent* to indicate how you want to specify the table's width.

4. Type the measurement into the text box next to Specify Width.

5. Click OK.

For example, if you select Specify Width, type **80** as the value, and choose in Percent as the unit of measurement, the table fills 80 percent of the width of the page.

Positioning a table

You can also position a table between the left and right margins. To do so, you use the Table Properties box once again. Here are the exact steps:

1. Right-click anywhere within the table that you want to position and then choose Table Properties from the menu that appears. The Table Properties dialog box appears.

2. Under Layout, choose an option from the Alignment drop-down list. Your options are as follows:

   Default: Typically, this option is the same as Left.

   Left: The left edge of the table aligns with the left margin of the page.

   Center: The table is centered between the page's left and right margins.

   Right: The right edge of the table aligns with the right edge of the page.

3. Make your selection and click OK. The table is repositioned in your page.

Showing and hiding borders

You can adjust the width of your table's borders at any time by using the table Border Size property. If you set the border size to zero (0), no borders are visible. In FrontPage Express, you still see the dotted lines that represent the borders, and the content within the table is still aligned as though the borders are there, as shown in the top half of Figure 6-4. If you set the Border Size to 1, a single thin line — exactly one pixel in width — separates the cells of the table. If you set the Border size to 2 or greater, the lines are visible and the outermost borders take on a three-dimensional look, as shown at the bottom of Figure 6-4.

To set the border width in your own table, follow these steps:

1. Right-click the table and choose Table Properties to bring up the Table Properties dialog box.

2. Adjust the Border Size option to the width of your choosing.

3. Click OK.

Figure 6-4:   Examples of a table Border Size property.

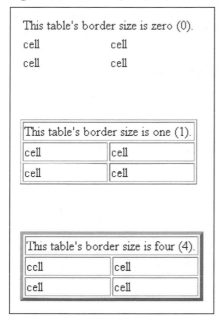

This table's border size is zero (0).

cell   cell

cell   cell

This table's border size is one (1).	
cell	cell
cell	cell

This table's border size is four (4).	
cell	cell
cell	cell

Coloring borders

If your table has visible borders, you can determine the color(s) you want those borders to be. Here's how:

1. Right-click anywhere in the table and choose Table Properties to bring up the Table Properties dialog box.

2. Under Custom Colors, choose a color from the Border drop-down list.

3. (Optional) If you want to color the inner and outer edges of the three-dimensional border independently, choose the colors you want from the Light Border and Dark Border drop-down lists.

4. Click OK.

To color the border around a single cell in a table, right-click that cell, choose Cell Properties, and then choose a background color from the Cell Properties dialog box that appears.

Coloring the background

You can also color the background of the table or even use a picture as the table's background. Just follow these steps:

1. Right-click the Table and choose Table Properties to open the Table Properties dialog box.

2. (Optional) Choose a color for the table's background by selecting a color from the Background Color drop-down list.

3. (Optional) Choose a graphic image for the table's background by selecting the Use Background Image option. Then use the Browse button to open the graphic image that you want to act as the table's background.

Be aware that not all Web browsers can display a background picture. So you may want to choose both a color and a background image, if you have an image available. That way, if the image doesn't show in a specific browser, the table's background color still shows through.

If you want to color just one or more cells, select the cell(s) you want to color. Right-click the selection, choose Cell Properties (*not* Table Properties), and then choose an option from the Background Color drop-down list. I discuss techniques for selecting cells in the next section.

Adding and Deleting Cells

A table is never set in concrete. You can change the size, appearance, and position of the table at any time. You can also format individual rows, columns, and cells to your liking. To do that kind of formatting, you first need to figure out how to select the cells, rows, or columns you want to work with.

Selecting cells, rows, and columns

Selecting cells in a table is usually easy because you have many different ways to do it. You can just use whatever technique is most convenient at the moment.

- To select a single cell, move the cursor into that cell and choose Table⇨Select Cell from the menu bar.

- To select a row, move the cursor into any cell within the row and choose Table⇨Select Row from the menu bar.

- To select multiple rows, move the mouse pointer to the table's leftmost border, starting at the first or the last row you want to select. The mouse pointer turns to a small black arrow when the cursor is right on the table border. Drag the small black arrow up or down to select multiple rows.

- To select a column, move the cursor into any cell within the row and choose Table⇨Select Column from the menu bar.

- To select multiple columns, move the mouse pointer to the table's outermost table border, starting at the top of the first or last column you want to select. The mouse pointer turns to a small black arrow when the cursor is right on the table border. Drag the small black arrow to the left or right to select multiple columns.

- To select all the cells in a table, move the cursor anywhere within the table and choose Table⇨Select Table.

- To deselect any cells in a selection area, hold down the Ctrl key and click the cell that you want to deselect.

- To select some of the cells in a row or column, or a group of cells within the table, first select the entire row or column (or several rows and columns). Then deselect some of the cells by holding down the Ctrl key and clicking the cells that you want to deselect.

If you select too many cells and want to start over, you can easily deselect all the currently selected cells. Just click anywhere within the table or press one of the cursor-positioning keys.

Adding rows and columns

If at any time you need to add more rows or columns to your table, you have a couple ways to do so. If you simply want to add a new row to the bottom of the table, move the cursor to the table's last cell (the cell in the lower-right corner). Then press the Tab key.

If you want to add columns or insert multiple rows or columns within the table, follow these steps:

1. To add a new row anywhere within the table, move the cursor to the spot where you want to insert a row or column.

2. Choose Table⇨Insert Rows or Columns from the FrontPage Express menu bar. The Insert Rows or Columns dialog box appears.

3. Choose either Columns or Rows to indicate which you want to add.

4. Choose the number of rows or columns that you want to add.

5. If you're adding rows, choose Above Selection or Below Selection, or if you're inserting columns, choose Left of Selection or Right of Selection, depending on where you want to insert the rows or columns in relation to the cursor position within the table.

6. Click OK.

Deleting rows and columns

To delete a row or column, follow these steps:

1. Select the row(s) or column(s) you want to delete.

2. Press the Delete key.

If you bite off more than you intended, choose Edit⇨Undo Clear to bring back the row(s) or column(s).

To delete an entire table, move the cursor to any spot within the table and select Table⇨Select Table. Then press the Delete key.

Merging and Splitting Cells

The largest cell in any table row or column generally determines the height and width of that table row or column. If you put a large picture into a table cell, the entire row must become as large as the picture. To get around this problem, you can *merge* two or more smaller cells to make a larger cell. You can also *split* any single cell into two or more smaller cells. You can merge or split cells either before or after filling them. So as with everything else in FrontPage Express, you can change the cells to better fit the table's contents. The following basic steps summarize how to merge and split cells:

1. Select the two or more cells that you want to merge into a larger, single cell. Or move the cursor into the single cell that you want to split into two or more smaller cells.

2. Choose one of the following options:

To merge the selected cells into a single cell, choose Table⇨Merge Cells from the menu bar.

To split the single cell into two or more cells, choose Table⇨Split Cells from the menu bar.

For example, suppose you have a picture of an orchid that you want to add to the sample table created in the commonorchids.htm page. You want this picture to appear within the first column of the table and span the entire height of the table. The first step is to select all cells in the first column either by clicking at the very top of the column or by choosing Table⇨Select Column from the menu bar. Then choose Table⇨Merge Cells to merge the selected cells into one, as shown in Figure 6-5.

Figure 6-5: Cells in the first column are merged into one tall cell.

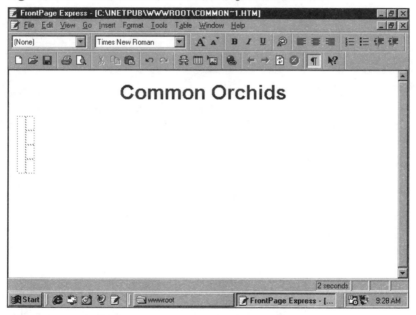

Filling a Table

A table cell can contain any text or picture. Filling a table cell is pretty easy. Just follow these steps:

1. Move the cursor to the cell you want to fill, either by clicking that cell or by using the cursor-positioning keys to move the cursor to the cell.

2. Choose one of the following options:

To add text to the table, simply type your text normally.

To add a picture, click the Insert Image button on the toolbar or choose Insert⇨Image from the menu bar. Then insert the image normally, as described in Chapter 4.

The cell's size automatically adjusts to accommodate whatever text or picture you put into the cell. Don't worry about precisely sizing the cell right away. As you fill cells in the table, the cells, columns, and rows automatically adjust to best fit all the contents of the table. If you don't like the appearance of the table after you fill all the cells, you can make changes (as I discuss later in this chapter).

When typing in a table cell, be aware that pressing the Enter key causes a large gap between the typed lines and makes the entire row quite tall. To fix the problem, press the Backspace key to delete the invisible carriage-returns. If you really want to type two or more lines of text into a table cell, and you want to specify exactly where each line breaks, press Shift+Enter (rather than just Enter) to insert a line break with no extra spacing.

As an example of filling a table, Figure 6-6 shows you the sample table after insertion of a graphic image into the large upper-left cell created by merging three cells together. To type text into the remaining cells, simply position the cursor in the cell and type the text shown. At no time press the Enter key. Format the text at the top of the second column as a Heading 2, which changes the text to the large size and italics. The remaining text is normal size and some in boldface.

Figure 6-6: The sample table with a picture and some text typed in.

```
FrontPage Express - [C:\INETPUB\WWWROOT\COMMON~1.HTM]
File  Edit  View  Go  Insert  Format  Tools  Table  Window  Help
[None]          Times New Roman
```

Common Orchids

Cattleya amethystoglossa

Origin: Brazil

Flowers in: Autumn/winter

Flower size: 4-5 in.

```
6 seconds
Start        wwwroot        FrontPage Express - [...        9:30 AM
```

Tip

You can format the text within a table and even convert text to hyperlinks by using the techniques described in previous chapters.

Aligning Cell Contents

Text and pictures within table cells can be aligned inside the cell. The top half of Figure 6-7 shows examples of horizontal alignment. You see the text and picture left-aligned, centered, and right-aligned within their cells. If a particular cell is taller than the contents displayed within that cell, you can also adjust the horizontal alignment of the contents. In the bottom half of Figure 6-7, the first cell of the row contains a picture that in turn makes all the cells in that row quite tall. The text to the right of the picture shows examples of vertical alignment. You see the text top-aligned, middle-aligned, and bottom-aligned within its tall cell.

Figure 6-7: Examples of aligning a cell's contents.

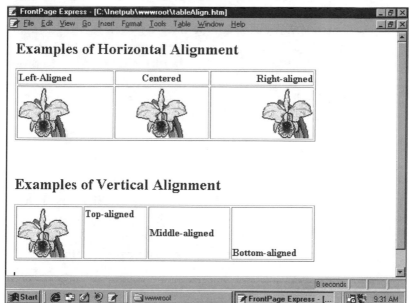

To align the contents of a table's cell within the cell, follow these steps:

1. Move the cursor to the text that you want to align. Or if you want to align the contents of several cells, select those cells.

2. Choose Table⇨Cell Properties from the FrontPage Express menu bar. The Cell Properties dialog box appears.

3. Choose an option from the Horizontal Alignment and/or Vertical Alignment drop-down list.

4. Click OK to close the Cell Properties dialog box.

Keep in mind that the distance between a cell's border and its contents is determined by the Cell Padding option. For example, if the cell padding is set to five pixels and you right-align text in that cell, a five-pixel gap appears between the end of the text and the cell's border. Cell padding is a property of the entire table, so you can't adjust the padding for a single cell or group of cells. To adjust the padding, right-click the table, choose Table Properties, and make your selection from the Cell Padding option in the Table Properties dialog box that appears.

With your new skill at creating tables, you have great control over the appearance of your Web pages. In the next chapter, you discover how to publish your pages by uploading them to your Web server. After that's done, you and everyone else on the Internet can see your pages via the Web.

CHAPTER 7

PUBLISHING AND PROMOTING YOUR SITE

IN THIS CHAPTER

- ■ Discovering what you need from your Web host
- ■ Using the Web Publishing Wizard
- ■ Visiting your own site
- ■ Promoting your site

When you're happy with the Web pages you create on your PC and you're ready to show them to the world, you need to *upload* (copy) those pages to your Web presence provider's Web server. Unfortunately, each Web presence provider (WPP) has its own unique way of doing things. You need to get that information directly from your WPP. Nonetheless, this chapter gives you a general understanding of how the process works with most WPPs by showing you one method of uploading pages.

Getting What You Need from Your WPP

Your Web server account undoubtedly resides on a computer that's accessible through the Internet and has its own URL. The URL that you use to *publish* your site may be different from the URL that other people on the Internet use to visit your site. To prevent people from changing your Web site without your permission, you receive a user name and password from your WPP. When you jot down the URL, user name, and password that your WPP provides, be sure to use exactly the same uppercase and lowercase letters that they do, because these things are usually case-sensitive.

Don't assume that the user name and password for publishing your Web pages are the same as the user name and password you use to log onto your Internet service provider (ISP). They're probably different. To upload pages to your Web server, you need the user name and password from your Web presence provider. Even if your ISP *is* your WPP, you may still need a separate user name and password to load pages onto the Web server.

Also, different WPPs offer different protocols for uploading pages. A *protocol* is a set of rules that defines how the data is sent across the network. For example, the Internet supports HTTP (HyperText Transfer Protocol), the protocol used for sending Web pages across the Internet. The Internet also supports FTP (File Transfer Protocol), which is generally used just for transferring files over the Internet without viewing them. If your WPP offers FrontPage Server Extensions, you may not need to use any of these protocols because the Web Publishing Wizard, described a little later in this chapter, can detect the appropriate protocol automatically.

So, only your WPP can give you the information you need to upload your Web pages to their Web server. After you gather the necessary information, jot it down in the third column of Table 7-1, which also shows examples of how the information may look. If your ISP doesn't provide you with information about the directory to publish to or the protocol, chances are you don't need that information to publish your pages.

Table 7-1: Information You Need from Your WPP to Publish your Pages

Info from WPP Notes	*Example*	*Write Yours Here*
URL to publish to	`http://crash.cts.com`	
Directory to publish to*	`/u5/alan/public_html`	
User name	AlanS	
Password	wangdoodle	
Protocol*	FTP	

*Not required by all WPPs. Leave blank if your WPP doesn't provide this information.

Using the Web Publishing Wizard

The Web Publishing Wizard (see Chapter 1 for installation instructions) is probably the easiest tool for uploading pages to your Web server. I can't guarantee that it works with all Web servers, but it's certainly worth a try. To use the Web Publishing Wizard, first make sure that you close FrontPage Express and save all your Web pages. Then follow these steps, starting from the Windows desktop:

1. Choose Start⇨Programs⇨Internet Explorer⇨Web Publishing Wizard. If you can't find the Web Publishing Wizard there, try choosing Start⇨Programs⇨Accessories⇨Internet Tools to get to the wizard.

2. Read the first page of the wizard and then click Next. The next wizard page, titled Select A File Or Folder appears.

3. Enter the path to the local folder that contains all your Web pages and graphics. The path should be

C:\Inetpub\wwwroot. Then make sure that the Include
subfolders check box is selected, as shown in Figure 7-1.

Figure 7-1:   Specify your local Web folder in this page of the wizard.

4. Click Next. If this is your first time using Web
   Publishing Wizard, you're taken to a page titled Name
   The Web Server. Go to Step 5 now. On the other hand,
   if you've used the Web Publishing Wizard in the past and
   have already defined your Web server, you're taken to a
   page titled Select Your Web Server. In this case, choose
   the name of your Web server from the drop-down list,
   and then skip to Step 8.

5. Type a simple descriptive name for this Web server. You
   can use the name of your WPP or whatever you like. You
   don't need to enter a URL here.

6. Click Next. The Specify the URL and Directory page
   appears.

7. Type the URL exactly as provided by your ISP. If your ISP also gives you the name of a specific directory to publish to, you need to include that information at the end of the URL, preceded by a slash. As you see in Figure 7-2, I specified both the URL and directory name examples used in Table 7-1 earlier in this chapter. Leave the second text box showing your local C:\Inetpub\ wwwroot folder.

Figure 7-2:   The first text box shows your Web server and possibly the directory that you publish to at that server.

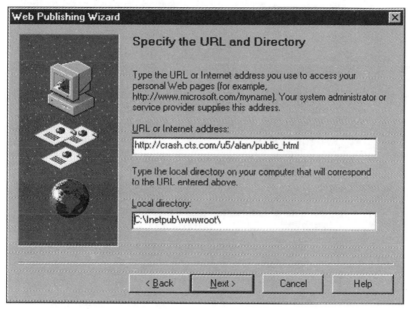

8. Click Next.

What happens next depends on several circumstances. Basically, you need to follow the instructions that each page of the wizard presents, clicking the Next or Finish button after reading the page and filling in any blanks. At some point, you see a dialog box asking for your user name and password.

Be sure to fill in the information provided by your WPP using exactly the same uppercase and lowercase letters.

After you click OK, the wizard may take a few seconds to verify your user name and password against the server. If the wizard can detect the protocol expected by your Web server, the wizard starts uploading pages right away. If the wizard can't detect the necessary protocol, the Specify a Service Provider page appears. If that happens, click Next and choose a protocol, such as FTP, from the Service Provider drop-down list. Then click Next again. Keep doing so until you get to the final page, where you can click the Finish button to start the upload.

After you successfully fill in all the blanks that Web Publishing Wizard requires, you see a dialog box with a progress meter that tells you how the transfer is going. When the transfer is complete, you see a message telling you so. Just click OK to close the Wizard. Then skip to the "Browsing Your Own Page" section later in this chapter.

If you have any problems with Web Publishing Wizard, first try repeating the preceding steps, checking carefully to make sure that you're entering all the information provided by your ISP correctly. If problems persist, you have two choices:

■ Contact your WPP, tell someone there that you're trying to upload your pages using the Microsoft Web Publishing Wizard, and ask the person to provide assistance.

■ Forget about using the Web Publishing Wizard and instead follow whatever instructions your WPP provides for uploading your pages.

Unfortunately, the preceding information is a little vague. But because no two WPPs are exactly alike, I can't really make the information any more specific. Getting pages uploaded to a

Web server can be a frustrating experience. Often it takes quite a bit of communication with your WPP to get the job done.

Many WPPs support the use of FTP as the protocol for uploading pages. If you need to go shopping for a good Windows FTP program, try the Ipswitch WS_FTP Pro. You can download a free shareware evaluation copy of that program from www.ipswitch.com. That same Web site also contains documentation for using the WS_FTP Pro program.

Browsing Your Own Page

After you successfully upload your Web pages to your Web server, you may want to make sure that your home page is accessible at the URL provided by your WPP. This URL is the one the general public uses to view your site and is likely to look something like this:

```
www.yourIsp.com/~yourName
```

Or like this:

```
www.yourIsp.com/yourName
```

Simply enter that URL into your Web browser and then press Enter to display your home page, exactly as anyone else on the Internet sees it.

You may have to wait a couple of seconds, but eventually your home page should appear in your browser. To test your links, click any hyperlink that's available on your Web page. To return to your home page after visiting another page in your site, click the Back button of your Web browser.

Changing Your Pages

After you upload your pages to a Web server, keep in mind that you have two copies of each file in your site. One copy remains in your C:\Inetub\wwwroot folder; the other copy is on the Web server. When you make changes or corrections to your pages, do so on your local PC. But don't forget to publish your pages again after making those changes. Otherwise, people visiting your site on the Internet won't see any of those changes and corrections!

Promoting Your Web Site

After your Web site becomes available on the Web, you need to let people know about it if you're going to get any traffic. Most people include their Web site's URL on business cards, on letterhead, in ads they print, and so forth. You can certainly do the same. You may also want to make sure that people searching the Web through search engines like Yahoo! and Excite can find your pages. Most of the large search engines automatically scour the Internet for Web pages and add them to their databases automatically. So even if you do nothing to promote your site, your pages may eventually end up in those search engines anyway.

However, you can do a few things to get your pages listed sooner and perhaps more accurately. One thing you can do is add a series of `<meta>` tags (called meta tags) to the head section of each page. The following list summarizes the tags you use for promotion:

- **Title:** Represents the title of your page as you want it to appear within the search engine.

- **Description:** A description of the page's contents, visible in many Web browsers.

- **Keywords:** A list of individual words that the search engine uses to index your page. When a search engine's user enters a word that matches one of your keywords, your page is included in the search results.

Some search engines actually index every word in your Web page (excluding words like *the* and *a*). But including a list of keywords in your meta tags is still a good idea. Follow these steps to add meta tags to a Web page:

1. In FrontPage Express, open the page to which you want to add meta tags. At the very least, you want to add these tags to your home page.

2. Choose File⇨Page Properties from the FrontPage Express menu bar. The Page Properties dialog box appears.

3. Click the Custom tab.

4. Click the Add button in the lower half of the dialog box under User Variables.

5. Under Name, type the word **title**, **description**, or **keywords**, depending on which tag you want to enter.

6. Under value, type your page title, description, or keywords, depending on which word you typed in as the name.

7. Click OK.

8. Repeat Steps 4 through 7 until you add all three tags.

Figure 7-3 shows the addition of title, description, and keywords to the Orchid Club Home Page, index.html. As you see in the dialog box, you also can easily modify or remove a tag by clicking it and then clicking one of the buttons to the right of the tags. When you're satisfied with your tags, just click OK at the bottom of the dialog box to save the changes.

Figure 7-3: Meta tags for title, description, and keywords added to the page.

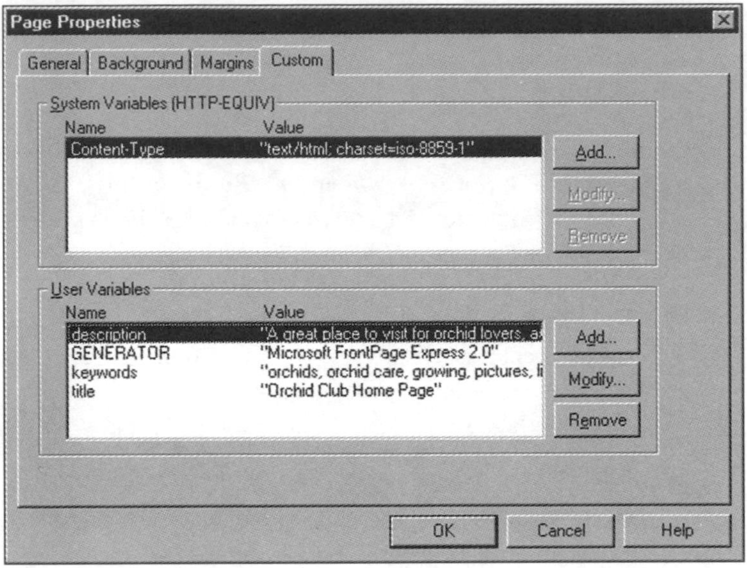

Don't forget to save and close the page. Also, keep in mind that you've only made the changes on your local PC. To copy the modified page to your Web server, go through whatever normal routine you use to upload your pages to your Web server.

Adding your URL to search engines

If you don't want to wait around for search engines to stumble upon your Web site, you can speed things along by adding the site yourself. Typically, this procedure involves visiting the search engine that you want to add your site to and then digging around the site to find an Add URL or Submit Your Site link. Following the link should take you to instructions and a form for submitting your site. Typically, all you have to do is type in your site's URL. The search engine goes (eventually) to your site and adds your site to its database.

To get you started, Table 7-2 lists some of the major search engines and the URL of the page you use for adding your site. Be aware, however, that the URLs may change. So if you don't find the Add URL page at the URL given, go to the search engine's home page and look around for a link to the new page for adding sites.

Table 7-2: Popular Search Engines and the URLs of Pages for Adding Your Site

Engine	Add URL Page
AltaVista	www.altavista.com/av/content/addurl.htm
AOL Netfind	www.aol.com/netfind/info/addyoursite.html
Excite	www.excite.com/info/add_url
HotBot	www.hotbot.com/addurl.asp
LookSmart	www.looksmart.com/aboutus/partners/subsite.html
WebCrawler	www.Webcrawler.com/info/add_url
Yahoo!	www.yahoo.com/info/suggest

Using submission services

If you prefer to spend money rather than time to promote your Web site on the Internet, plenty of promotion services on the Internet are glad to do that for you. Generally, these services are a cost-effective means of promoting your site because they use custom software to add your site to all the major search engines, plus dozens, or even hundreds, of smaller engines. Costs vary a great deal, so you want to shop around. If you simply use your Web browser to pull up any major search engine and then search for "Web promotion" or "Web site promotion," you can find links to many such services.

CLIFFSNOTES REVIEW

Use this CliffsNotes Review to practice what you've learned in this book and to build your confidence in doing the job right the first time. After you work through the review questions, the problem-solving exercises, and the fun and useful practice projects, you're well on your way to achieving your goal of publishing your first Web page.

Q&A

1. When you save a page and give it a title in the Save As dialog box, where does the title appear?

    a. In the title bar of most Web browsers

    b. At the top of your page

    c. In the status bar at the bottom of most Web browsers

2. Suppose you insert a list, graphic image, line, or other element into your page and then decide to change its appearance. Describe the technique you can use in FrontPage Express to alter the item's properties.

    _____

    _____

3. Which of the following can you accomplish by adding a hyper-link to your Web page?

    a. Let visitors jump to another Web page

    b. Let visitors type an e-mail message that's preaddressed to you

    c. Let visitors download files

    d. All of the above

4. If you have problems uploading your Web pages to a server, which of the following would be your best resource for finding solutions to the problem?

    a. Microsoft Tech Support

    b. Your Web presence provider

    c. The www.cliffsnotes.com Web site

    d. Your computer's manufacturer

5. Name two types of form fields that enable a user to select only one item from a set of mutually exclusive options.

_____

_____

6. Which program is specifically designed to help you upload your Web pages to a Web server?

    a. FrontPage Express

    b. Personal Web Server

    c. Web Publishing Wizard

    d. FrontPage 2000

Answers: (1) a. (2) Right-click the item and choose the appropriate Properties option from the menu that appears. (3) d. (4) b. (5) Radio buttons, drop-down list. (6) c.

Scenarios

1. You're browsing Web sites that offer free graphic images that you can use in your Web site. You find an image you want to use, so you need to copy it to your local hard drive. Explain how you would do that.

_____

_____

2. You place a hyperlink in your Web page. But when you test the link, you discover that you must have made a mistake because the link doesn't work. Explain how you can change the link in FrontPage Express.

_____

_____

Answers: (1) Right-click the Image and choose Save Picture As. (2) Right-click the hyperlink and choose Hyperlink Properties.

Consider This

■ Did you know that as an alternative to using Insert⇨Horizontal Line to insert a line into your page, you can use a graphic image as a line? You can find such graphic images at many of the Web sites listed at `http://best-of-Web.com/computer/clipart_index.shtml`. See Chapter 4 for information on downloading images and inserting them into your Web page.

■ Did you know you can place left-aligned, centered, and right-aligned text onto a single line in FrontPage Express? You can't do so if you try using menu commands or toolbar buttons. Instead, you insert a table containing one row and three columns into your page and then size the table to 100 percent of the page width. Type text into each of the three cells. Set the horizontal alignment of the center cell to Center and the horizontal alignment of the right-most cell to Right. See Chapter 6 if you need help with that.

■ Did you know that you can divide your Web page into multiple columns and give each column its own background color? Create a table that contains as many columns as you want the page to have. To give each column a specific width and color, select a column, right-click it, and choose Cell Properties. Give the column a width in pixels and a background color. You can then enter text, hyperlinks, and graphic images into each column individually. The cell grows in height to accommodate whatever you enter, giving the appearance of columns in a page.

Practice Project

A visitor is so impressed with your Web site that she asks you to create a site for her, extolling the virtues of owning Koi fish. Follow these steps:

1. Open your C:\Inetpub\wwwroot folder from Windows and then right-click within that folder to create a new folder named Koi.

2. Start Microsoft Front Page and on a blank page type **Koi Pond**. Format the text as Heading 1 and center it.

3. Save the new page to http:**//yourcomputername/**koi/index.html, replacing yourcomputername with the name of your computer.

4. Close FrontPage Express and any other open windows. Then start up your Web browser and browse to http://yourcomputername/koi.

5. Use your Web browser and favorite search engine to research sites about Koi fish to get ideas, information, and any free graphics you can use in your site. Save any useful pictures to your C:\Inetpub\wwwroot\koi folder.

6. Reopen FrontPage Express, open your C:\Inetpub\wwwroot\koi\index.html page, and add text and pictures to complete the page. Be creative — this is your creation. Just remember to keep all files for this site in your C:\Inetpub\wwwroot\koi folder, so they remain separate from your other site's files.

7. When uploading the site to a Web server, be sure to upload all the files in that C:\Inetpub\wwwroot\koi folder.

CLIFFSNOTES
RESOURCE CENTER

The learning doesn't need to stop here. CliffsNotes Resource Center shows you the best of the best — links to the best information in print and online about publishing on the Web. Look for these terrific resources at your favorite bookstore or local library and on the Internet. When you're online, make your first stop www.cliffsnotes.com, where you can find even more useful information about Web publishing.

Books

This CliffsNotes book is one of many great books on Web publishing from IDG Books Worldwide, Inc. So if you want some great next-step books, check out some of these other publications:

HTML 4 Bible, by Bryan Pfaffenberger and Alexis D. Gutzman, is an excellent book for gaining in-depth knowledge of HTML. You also find out about image maps and forms in detail. This book also introduces JavaScript and Cascading Style Sheets. IDG Books Worldwide, Inc. $49.99.

JavaScript For Dummies, 2nd Edition, by Emily A. Vander Veer, is a great way for nonprogrammers to learn how to add the power of JavaScript to their Web pages. The book includes a CD. IDG Books Worldwide, Inc. $29.99.

Microsoft FrontPage 2000 Bible, by David Elderbrock and David Karlins, is a must-have when you're planning on moving up to FrontPage 2000 to create more sophisticated Web sites. The skills you gained from this book will carry over beautifully. IDG Books Worldwide, Inc. $39.99.

Roger C. Parker's Guide to Web Content and Design, by Roger C. Parker, covers choosing a Web site address, developing quality content, engaging your visitors, promoting your Web site, providing customer service, and more. This book demonstrates how you can maximize your commercial forays onto the Internet. IDG Books Worldwide, Inc. $39.95.

You can easily find books published by IDG Books Worldwide, Inc., in your favorite bookstores, at the library, on the Internet, and at a store near you. We also have three Web sites that you can use to read about all the books we publish:

www.cliffsnotes.com

www.dummies.com

www.idgbooks.com

Internet

Check out these Web sites for more information on creating Web pages, gathering graphic images and multimedia files, and publishing and promoting your Web site.

Coolnerds.com, www.coolnerds.com/author, is author Alan Simpson's site, offering tons of resources for aspiring and accomplished Web site developers, including quick links to all the best online authoring references, tutorials, and free graphic images.

NCSA's A Beginners Guide to HTML, www.ncsa. uiuc.edu/General/Internet/WWW, can help you figure out what's going on when you're ready to start deciphering all the tags that FrontPage Express creates for you.

SubmitIt, www.submitit.com, takes the headache out of submitting your Web pages to search engines one site at a time. Their program submits your site to over 400 search engines and directories and provides tools for verifying your site's placement.

The Official Microsoft Home Page for FrontPage, www.microsoft.com/frontpage, is the Microsoft home page for the FrontPage Express big brother, FrontPage 2000. This site includes downloads, multimedia demos, and just about anything else you need to help you decide whether or not to purchase the product.

The Sound Ring Home Site, www.alexcia.com, is the home of the Sound Ring, with links to tons of free MIDI and WAV files that you can use to add music and sounds to your web site.

The Whole Internet Guide to Clip Art, http://best-of-web.com/computer/clipart_index.shtml, is the place to go when you're looking for some freebie graphic images to embellish your Web site. This site contains links to all the best image repositories.

Web Affiliate Programs, www.webaffiliateprograms. com, is a great resource for those looking to generate income from a Web site without going to the trouble of building an online store.

Next time you're on the Internet, don't forget to drop by www.cliffsnotes.com. We created an online Resource Center that you can use today, tomorrow, and beyond.

Magazines and Other Media

To keep up with advances in all aspects of publishing on the Web, check out these periodicals:

Web Developer's Journal, webdevelopersjournal.com, is an online magazine geared toward all aspects of creating and maintaining Web sites.

Web Techniques, www.webtechniques.com, is an excellent magazine for keeping in touch with advances in all aspects of Web development. Free subscription to qualifying Internet professionals, $34.95 annually for nonprofessionals.

Send Us Your Favorite Tips

In your quest for knowledge, have you ever experienced that sublime moment when you figure out a trick that saves time or trouble? Perhaps you realized you were taking ten steps to accomplish something that could take two. Or you found a little-known workaround that achieved great results. If you've discovered a useful tip that helped you create a Web page more effectively, and you'd like to share it, the CliffsNotes staff would love to hear from you. Go to our Web site at www.cliffsnotes.com and look for the Talk to Us button. If we select your tip, we may publish it as part of *CliffsNotes Daily*, our exciting, free e-mail newsletter. To find out more, or to subscribe to the newsletter, go to www.cliffsnotes.com on the Web.

INDEX

COMING SOON FROM CLIFFSNOTES

Online Shopping

HTML

Choosing a PC

Beginning Programming

Careers

Windows 98 Home Networking

eBay Online Auctions

PC Upgrade and Repair

Business

Microsoft Word 2000

Microsoft PowerPoint 2000

Finance

Microsoft Outlook 2000

Digital Photography

Palm Computing

Investing

Windows 2000

Online Research

COMING SOON FROM CLIFFSNOTES
Buying and Selling on eBay

Have you ever experienced the thrill of finding an incredible bargain at a specialty store or been amazed at what people are willing to pay for things that you might toss in the garbage? If so, then you'll want to learn about eBay — the hottest auction site on the Internet. And CliffsNotes *Buying and Selling on eBay* is the shortest distance to eBay proficiency. You'll learn how to:

- Find what you're looking for, from antique toys to classic cars

- Watch the auctions strategically and place bids at the right time

- Sell items online at the eBay site

- Make the items you sell attractive to prospective bidders

- Protect yourself from fraud

Here's an example of how the step-by-step CliffsNotes learning process simplifies placing a bid at eBay:

1. Scroll to the Web page form that is located at the bottom of the page on which the auction item itself is presented.

2. Enter your registered eBay username and password and enter the amount you want to bid. A Web page appears that lets you review your bid before you actually submit it to eBay. After you're satisfied with your bid, click the Place Bid button.

3. Click the Back button on your browser until you return to the auction listing page. Then choose View⇨Reload (Netscape Navigator) or View⇨Refresh (Microsoft Internet Explorer) to reload the Web page information. Your new high bid appears on the Web page, and your name appears as the high bidder.